Andrew Glass

**Poems and songs**

Andrew Glass

**Poems and songs**

ISBN/EAN: 9783744770682

Printed in Europe, USA, Canada, Australia, Japan

Cover: Foto ©Thomas Meinert / pixelio.de

More available books at **www.hansebooks.com**

# POEMS AND SONGS.

BY

ANDREW GLASS.

AYR:
Printed and Published for the Author by
HENRY AND GRANT.
MDCCCLXIX.

LOAN STACK

TO

# KENNEDY BROWN, ESQ., GIRVAN,

 This Volume

IS RESPECTFULLY DEDICATED, AS A GRATEFUL TRIBUTE FOR

MANY ACTS OF KINDNESS RENDERED TO

THE AUTHOR.

# PREFACE.

NEARLY all the Poems and Songs contained in this Volume have from time to time appeared in the columns of Ayrshire Newspapers. Many of them were hurriedly written, and lack that polish so essential to true Poetry; but, at the solicitation of many friends, I have been induced to publish them in the present form. Those who peruse this Book to discover imperfections will find many; but as some of the Pieces refer to places in the County endeared by many a fond recollection, and as the vale of the Girvan has been unsung by a nobler Poet, such considerations, despite its imperfections, were the chief reasons for inducing me to accede to a request so highly gratifying.

The measure of success that has been vouchsafed, even previous to publication, is a source of much satisfaction; and I would be destitute of a proper feeling of gratitude did I not warmly thank all those who have already thought so much of these stray effusions as to subscribe for my unpretending Volume.

ANDREW GLASS.

AYR, *March*, 1869.

# CONTENTS.

|  | PAGE |
|---|---|
| SUNBEAMS, | 9 |
| THE SEA, | 12 |
| THE PRODIGAL, | 15 |
| IN MEMORIAM: WILLIAM BUCHANAN, | 18 |
| PENKILL AND GLENQUHAPLE, | 21 |
| GIRVAN WATER, | 25 |
| OLD DAILLY CHURCHYARD, | 29 |
| THE MONEY CRISIS, | 33 |
| THE CASTLEHILL, | 37 |
| LADY CATHCART'S LAMENT, | 41 |
| THE STREAMS, | 44 |
| HOLYROOD, | 47 |
| CAMREGGAN BURN, | 53 |
| SONG OF THE UNEMPLOYED, | 55 |
| SPRING, | 57 |
| IN MEMORIAM: LORD CLYDE, | 60 |
| A LAY TO SCOTLAND, | 63 |
| TO A ROBIN, | 66 |
| WINTER, | 68 |
| IN MEMORIAM: WILLIAM CLARK, | 71 |
| REST, | 73 |
| DEATH OF COL. BLAIR, OF BLAIRQUHAN, | 76 |
| LOVELY GALLOWAY, | 78 |

## CONTENTS.

| | PAGE |
|---|---|
| LINES ON ARRAN, | 81 |
| AS LOVE DESCENDS, | 83 |
| THE DANISH FLOWER, | 85 |
| BATTLE OF INKERMAN, | 87 |
| A WELCOME TO GARIBALDI, | 89 |
| AUTUMN, | 92 |
| THE LILIES OF THE FIELD, | 94 |
| SONG OF THE COMING YEAR, | 96 |
| A BIRTH-DAY SONG, | 99 |
| THANKS FOR THE LIFEBOAT, | 101 |
| ANNIE'S HEAVEN AN' MAIR TO ME, | 103 |
| GREENAN CASTLE, | 105 |
| IN MEMORIAM: CAPTAIN BLAKENEY, | 109 |
| BROUNSTONE CASTLE, | 112 |
| CRUGGLETON CASTLE, | 114 |
| ARDROSSAN CASTLE, | 116 |
| LINES ON THE MARRIAGE OF A DEAR FRIEND, | 118 |
| THE HARVEST MOON IS STREAMING, LOVE, | 120 |
| LINES ON THE DEATH OF A YOUNG LADY, | 122 |
| THE BONNY STREAMS O' AYRSHIRE, | 124 |
| BEAUTIFUL MAY, | 126 |
| DREAM OF THE LITTLE COTTON-PIECER, | 128 |
| PEACE, COLUMBIA! | 131 |
| THE EMIGRANT'S FAREWELL, | 134 |
| SONG OF THE CARRICK FISHERMAN, | 136 |
| THE SABBATH, | 138 |
| ON HEARING A MAVIS SING IN GLASGOW, | 141 |
| A FAREWELL, | 143 |
| ARDMILLAN BAY, | 145 |

# CONTENTS.

|  | PAGE |
|---|---|
| GLENDOUNE, | 147 |
| A WINTER STORM, | 149 |
| LINES SUGGESTED BY THE ARRIVAL OF LORD CLYDE, | 152 |
| ON THE DEATH OF THE REV. WILLIAM DILL, | 155 |
| BRITAIN'S VOLUNTEERS, | 157 |
| A CHRISTMAS CAROL, | 159 |
| THE SUN'S GANE TO REST, | 162 |
| SONG OF THE SHUTTLE, | 164 |
| OH! DNINA LEAVE FAIR SCOTIA'S SHORE, | 167 |
| LINES SUGGESTED BY THE CLOSING YEAR, | 169 |
| GRANU TO HER SON, | 176 |
| ARRAN, | 179 |
| LINES ON THE ERECTION OF GENERAL NEILL'S MONUMENT, | 181 |
| SUMMER, | 183 |
| ADDRESS OF LORD G—'S TENANTRY, | 186 |
| JEANIE MOFFAT, | 189 |
| LORD EGLINTON'S BIRTH-DAY, | 191 |
| PADDY'S HALLUCINATIONS, | 194 |
| THE SUN HAD PRESSED HIS OCEAN BED, | 197 |
| KILKERRAN'S BONNY BRAES, | 199 |
| LINES WRITTEN ON BURNS' ANNIVERSARY, | 201 |
| SHAM FIGHT AT POLLOC, | 204 |
| LINES WRITTEN ON THE OPENING OF GIRVAN RAILWAY, | 209 |
| LINES ON THE DEATH OF CAPTAIN WILSON, | 212 |
| THE COTTON FAMINE, | 214 |
| LINES ON A TOMBSTONE IN ARDROSSAN CEMETERY, | 216 |

# POEMS AND SONGS.

## SUNBEAMS.

Bright Sunbeams of Summer, O come back again,
And quaff the clear dew-drops that gleam on the plain.
The woodlands are weary of waiting on you,
And the bird you bring with you—the gladsome Cuckoo.
Arise o'er the mountains on valleys and fens,
Awaken the music that sleeps in the glens,
For since you departed they're joyless and bare,
And the winds wander through them with notes of despair.

Bright Sunbeams of Summer, say, where have you been
Since you danced with the butterflies here on the green?
Have you lit the Pacific and gazed on its isles,
And given their daughters your gladsomest smiles?

Or strayed where the roses of India bloom,
Through the valleys of Cashmere, and breathed their perfume?
Marched o'er the Sahara, and blazed on its sand,
And shone on the pyramids mighty and grand?

Bright Sunbeams of Summer, haste back to the North,
And call the poor child of the Esquimaux forth
To gaze on your glory and dance on the snow,
And forget in your radiance his winter of woe;
The icy chains sever that bind up the rills,
The snows of Creation sweep down from the hills,
And the avalanche loudly your glories will sing,
As it rolls down the mountains where darkness reigns king.

Bright Sunbeams of Summer, rejoicing the earth,
The land must be lovely that first gave you birth.
Ye fall on the forests and bathe them in green;
Ye fall on the rivers, like silver their sheen;
Ye fall on the ocean in glory untold,
And stream o'er its waters like torrents of gold;
Ye fall on the wilderness, lonely and drear,
And the flowers that lay scentless in fragrance appear.

Bright Sunbeams of Summer, ye enter the cell
Where the wretched, the outcast, the criminal dwell,
And shine on their fetters as fondly and fair
As if none but the purest and noblest were there.
Bright, brilliant, effulgent, ye come from above
To teach us the lesson that Heaven is Love;
For on cottage and castle, on hovel and hall,
On saint and on sinner ye equally fall.

Bright Sunbeams of Summer, ye herald the time
When love like your light shall pervade every clime,
Constraining the erring to come back again
To the fold of the Shepherd on Calvary slain,
Who came from the Source of the sunbeams above,
To ransom and lead us to mansions of love—
To chase the dark demon of sin far away
To the regions ne'er lit by the sunbeams of day.

## THE SEA.

#### SUGGESTED BY THE WRECK OF THE LONDON.

Sea! beautiful Sea, how sweet to stray
O'er the sunlit beach, on a summer day!
When the rippling waves on the golden shore
Are singing such dreamlike music o'er,
That echo is silent within his cave,
And the sea-gull sleeps on the glassy wave,
While the sailor boy longs for the breeze to come
That shall waft him back to his old loved home.


Sea! stormy Sea, how dread the roar
Of thy wintry waves on the rocky shore!
When the foam of their fury is flung on high
O'er the beetling crags which their wrath defy;

When the mermaids, dripping within their caves,
Look with affright on the yeasty waves;
And the hurricane's voice, in the rock-bound bay,
Is heard o'er the mountains far away.


Sea! boisterous Sea, when thy waves run high,
And lightnings drop from the murky sky,
When cloud o'er cloud in confusion is hurled,
Like the massive wreck of a mighty world—
Then the stately ship and her gallant crew
Shudder to try their strength with you;
For there's death to those who dare to brave
The might that rests in thy crested wave.


Sea! pitiless Sea, could'st thou not spare
That gallant ship with its freight so fair
Of women, and children, and men as brave
As e'er in thy waters found a grave?
Could their lofty courage not melt thy mood,
As serene on the storm-swept deck they stood;
And while fiends in the air were ringing their knell,
Replied with a prayer and a calm farewell?

Sea ! terrible Sea, retain you may
Such trophies won to the final day ;
But when earth is ended, and time is fled,
And thou art commanded to yield thy dead,
Then issuing forth from thy depths far down,
They shall rise to receive their immortal crown,
And look a last radiant look on thee,
As they pass to where there is " no more Sea."

## THE PRODIGAL.

I will arise and to my Father go;
   I long to see his face before I die;
When once he sees my wretchedness and woe,
   He may look on me with a pitying eye,—
Forgive his erring, poor, repentant son,
For all the foul transgressions he has done.


Here do I perish for the lack of bread,
   An outcast and a swineherd—oh my God!
How little did I dream when forth I fled
   From my dear Father's loving, blest abode,
That I would fall so low; I fain would eat
The husks the swine tread 'neath their unclean feet.

Ungrateful world! I gave you all I had—
    Health, wealth, and strength—and ye bestow to me
The liberty to starve—I'm surely mad!—
    Afar from home and sunlit Galilee:
I will go back and seek my Father's face,
He may assign to me a servant's place.

The meanest servants have enough of bread
    Who wear the livery of my youthful home,
While o'er me famine's sable wings are spread:
    I will return. O Sire, I come, I come!
Do with me as thou wilt; I ask no more
Than be the humblest servant at thy door.

Pale, wasted, and forlorn, he turned his face
    Towards the home where youth flew joyous by;
His Father watched each homeward, weary pace,
    With pity beaming in his anxious eye;
Ran forth and met him, wept, and kissed his son,
Ere well his homeward journey was begun.

"Against thee, Father, and kind Heaven," he said,
    "My sins have been of blackest, deepest dye;

Oh, let me be the humblest servant made,
   For as a son I did thy laws defy.
My many acts of disobedience prove
I am unworthy of thy heartfelt love."


"Bring hither shoes," the loving Father said,
   "And on his finger put a precious ring;
Son, on my bosom rest thy weary head,
   Till forth the richest robe my servants bring:
Let mirth and gladness through my halls resound,
My darling son was lost, but now is found!"

## IN MEMORIAM: WILLIAM BUCHANAN.

The Poet, Patriot, Politician—Friend
   Of all who needed sympathy or aid,
Has passed away—how sudden was his end!—
   To where despairing fears are all allayed—
   Within the silent tomb Buchanan's laid!


His star arose effulgent, but it set,
   Like many a brilliant one, in sudden gloom;
Alas! that genius should the light beget
   That often lures but to an early tomb,
   And leaves dull millions moping in their room.

Beside his grave I could sit down and weep:
  But what's my sorrow to BUCHANAN now?
His is the calm serenity of sleep,
  Mine but the aching heart and fevered brow,
  As o'er his early grave I sadly bow.

His pathos, satire, sentiment, and song,
  Were gifts that drifted him temptation near;
And as I tread the voiceless graves among,
  I think on all his trials, with a tear,
  And judge with charity one lov'd so dear.

A friend to truth—an enemy to cant—
  He held up to derision what was wrong;
Despising, to his injury, the rant
  That passes current with the thoughtless throng,
  And yet they lov'd him for his wit and song.

Had he but trimm'd his sails to catch the breeze
  That blows from lordly quarters—like some Priest—
He might have yet been living, at his ease,
  And holding in his Goschen fast and feast,
  Admir'd by many a worldly saint, at least.

But sycophancy never was his sin ;
    He feared its meanness more than want of bread.
The mighty mass of men were judged by him
    Not by their wealth, but by their heart and head :
    All, but the Panderer, lov'd whate'er he said.

Could I in characters eternal write
    A lasting epitaph, the words would be—
" Pure as the stars that gem the robes of night —
    Large as the treasures of the boundless sea—
    BUCHANAN's sympathies to all were free ! "

# PENKILL AND GLENQUHAPLE.

### A REMINISCENCE.

Sing not to me of classic streams,
   But of Glenquhaple's flowery dells;
They haunt me yet like pleasant dreams
   On which the memory fondly dwells,—
Its yellow broom and hazel trees,
I see them waving in the breeze.

I see its waters flashing bright
   When leaping o'er Knockgerrin linn,
I hear them singing with delight
   Their everlasting mountain hymn,
As past Penkill they sweep in pride,
To woo the Girvan as a bride.

Penkill! what visions of the past
   Thy name recalls to memory dear,

Before life's dream was overcast
    Even with the shadow of a fear—
When earth appeared a blest abode,
And life a long, bright joyous road.


Where are my merry comrades—where,
    Who woke the echoes of the glen?
Why am I left alone with care,
    At home a stranger among men?
And only in a rock or tree,
An old familiar form to see.


Penkill remains, but they are gone
    That through its loopholes wont to gaze;
Perhaps like me they're dreaming on
'Its hoary towers, Glenquhaple's braes,
And gathering, far beyond the seas,
Brown nuts, red rowans from its trees.


Some to Australia strayed afar;
    Some tried their fortune on the main;
Some followed Colin Campbell's star;
    Some found a grave on India's plain—

The wandering winds the requiem raves
Of some who lie beneath the waves.


And I am left, but not alone,
    Penkill's grey towers remain to me,
Reminding me in many a tone
    Of those I never more may see,
Who sat beside its tottering wall,
And sported in its roofless hall.


Earth! give me back the friends I love,
    And I will thank thee now with tears;
Oh! through Glenquhaple let us rove,
    And view the scenes of bygone years,—
And on its braes again we'll sing
Farewell to woe and wandering!


Home!—fairest, dearest spot on earth;
    Home!—when exiled we turn to thee;
Home!—who forgets its joyous hearth,
    The haunt of love, truth, amity?
Home!—though that place be bleak and bare,
Home, childhood's home, is ever fair!

Home!—many quit its hallowed shade
    In search of what they never find;
For gold—oft lost as soon as made—
    They leave the sacred spot behind,
Where love presides—best gift of God—
To cheer us on life's weary road.

With love, a cottage by a brook,
    In some fair glen, is better far
Than palaces, though grand the look,
    If won by fraud or deadly war.
If love lights up the humblest cot,
Then that's a holy, happy spot.

Sing then no more of lands afar,
    But of Glenquhaple's sunlit dells—
The towering peak, the giddy scaur,
    Australia's golden strand excels.
Fame, fortune, glory, idly beam,
To lure me from its mountain stream.

# GIRVAN WATER.

### A REMINISCENCE.

The silvery Tweed and Celtic Tay
   Resound in many a Scottish song,
But Girvan winds its unsung way
   By stately castles old and strong,
Whose lords have followed Britain's star
On flood and field in many a war.

Brave Blair, who fell on Inkerman,
   Endears its name to more than me,
And sets the Castle of Blairquhan
   In Scotland's crown of chivalry—
Long may its towers, fair Carrick's pride,
Be mirrored in its silvery tide.

Descending from its mountain throne,
    It laves Kilkerran's flowery land;
Then in its sweetest undertone
    It murmurs past Bargany grand;
And waters, ere it seeks the sea,
Killochan, ever dear to me.


And dear to all who love to see
    The forest's children waving high,
Who love a clover-scented lea
    Where flowerets bloom of every dye;
Or love to sit and idly dream
By Carrick's fairest mountain stream.


Killochan's towers are growing grey,
    But Girvan's stream is still as bright
As when at first it did display
    Its beauty to the God of Light—
Unclouded as the fancies wove
In boyhood's day, of fame and love.


Like western clouds with sunset tinged,
    Youth's dreams and joys have passed away,

And left the world with sadness fringed—
   Dark, dreary, as a wintry day:
I tremble at the coming blast,
If all the future's like the past.


Yet memory, faithful as the dove
   That seeks its woodland home to die,
Returns to seek the fount of love
   It first beheld in woman's eye:
And through the misty screen of years
A mother's loving face appears.


Where Girvan woos the azure tide,
   We hand in hand langsyne did stray,
And gazed upon the ocean wide,
   Great Ailsa looming far away:
Now wandering stars that light the wave
Are shining on her humble grave.


Why then remain when those are gone
   That guarded, loved, and taught me Truth,
Like Adam, fallen and alone,
   Still sighing for the bowers of youth:

My Eden vanished from the earth
When death descended on her hearth.

Tho' kindred links are rent in twain,
    Fair stream, thy bowers are dear to me;
Killochan's towers and flowery plain
    In wistful dreams I often see:
And Time will never dim their face,
Nor plant a rival in their place.

# OLD DAILLY CHURCHYARD.


Old Dailly, peaceful, sweet abode,
    Thy memory still is dear to me ;
Tho' years have fled since last I trod
    The precincts of thy sanctuary,
And watched the ravens idly spread
Their sable wings above the dead.

Tho' sycamores their branches wave
    Above the altar's roofless shrine ;
Tho' nettles spring from aisle and nave,
    And through the gables moonbeams shine ;—
Yet still I love the old grey walls,
Up which the ivy darkly crawls.

Oft have I sat beneath their shade,
    In dreamy mood, in years gone by,

And seen the worshippers arrayed
    Beneath the godly pastor's eye—
The rich, the poor, whose names are gone,
Even from the sad memorial stone.

On Sabbath morn, here old and young,
    From cot and castle, came to pray;
Here Zion's songs they sweetly sung;
    Now, all is silence and decay,
Except the stream that murmurs by
That spot, where generations lie.

And sadly yet it seems to sing
    The requiem of the martyr'd brave,
Who owned on earth no other king
    Than He who triumphed o'er the grave;—
The purchased blessings we partake
Of those who died for conscience' sake.

From every crevice seemed to speak
    A tongue that told a tale of yore—
How Semple, guiltless, godly, meek,
    Was slain for truth before the door—

When Pride and Prelacy combined
To chain the chainless human mind.

Within its shade the ashes lie
   Of knights, whose bright heraldic shields
And pennons proudly flaunted high,
   And glory reaped on battle-fields—
Cathcart, a name to Carrick dear,
Boyd and Dalrymple sleepeth here.

And here, unknown to fame, alas!
   Repose the friends I loved in youth;
The dewdrops trembling on the grass
   No purer are than was the truth
They taught to me in bygone years:
Now on their graves I look through tears.

Beneath the yew tree's sombre shade,
   Beside Penwhauple's mountain stream,
Where Summer's riches are displayed,
   And peace and beauty reign supreme,
They found—if not a sculptur'd tomb—
A flowery spot, a peaceful home.

Here nothing breaks the solitude,
    Except old Dailly's distant mill,
The cushat cooing in the wood,
    The music of the passing rill;
No other sounds than these intrude
Upon their silent dreamless mood.

Here would I lay my weary head,
    When ended is life's fitful dream,
And mingle with the spirits fled
    When stars light up Penwhauple's stream;—
The Old Kirk's hoary, ivied dome
Would give me what I seek—A HOME.

## THE MONEY CRISIS.

**SUGGESTED BY THE FAILURE OF THE WESTERN BANK.**

Hech sirs! the gowd is unco saut—
A "Money Crisis" some folk ca't;
'Tis sure tae scrimp the puir man's pat,
   My humble frien'—
They say the Western's no worth that:
   'Tis doon yestreen!

While Winter, wi' it's chilly frown,
Has cast its shadow o'er the town,
We stan', like Lear, without a crown,
   Exposed an' bare,
While giant Want is hov'ring round
   Wi' hungry glare.

Adversities, like flakes o' snaw,
Baith thick and fast upon us fa',
But sairest aye put to the wa'
   Is Labour's bairn—
Misfortune hauds him in her claw,
   Relentless, stern.


He has nae gear, alas! nor lan';
His bits o' claes gang tae the pawn;
He thinks against the stream tae stan';
   But doon he goes—
Anither victim tae a ban'
   O' ruthless foes.


A' this is caused by speculation,
Within a sae-ca'd Christian nation,
That lang has held the foremaist station
   For gear an' faith:
Noo everything's tae desolation
   For want o' baith!


Like decent Lot, frae Sodom gaun,
   They'll no tak' time tae speak or stan';

Gentility micht shake the han'
　　An' rest its shanks—
But on it's striding, like a man,
　　Tae drain the banks!

But aye ascending, here and there,
May still be heard a heartfelt prayer,
That in the bank they had nae mair,
　　Like mony ithers—
A groan is a' they ha'e tae spare
　　Tae luckless brithers.

Lord save us frae the hammer noo,
For times are lookin' unco blue,
Our granaries are burstin' fou,
　　Tae sell is ruin:
Lord, gie us time tae mix the new,
　　An' put the screw on!

But surely a' ye ha'e's no gane?
Ye still display a gowden chain,
An' linen fair, withoot a stain:
　　Ye're unco braw—

An' if ye but some time can gain,
    Ye'll manage a'.

But should a' fail, ye're no alane,
Just look at that bit ragged wean
That's chittering by a cauld hearthstane,
    Wi' want maist dead,
Whase faither's tae the sodgers gane
    For want o' bread.

Come cheer his sorrowing mither's heart,
And dinna act the Levite's part;
Ye hae the gowd—ye needna start!—
    Wad soothe her care,
An' mak the demon, Want, depart
    Back tae his lair.

By acting thus ye but fulfil
The mandates of kind Heaven's will;
You honour your dishonoured bill
    Upon the bank
That ever blesses good and ill
    Of every rank.

## THE CASTLE-HILL.

How fair looks Arran from the Castle-Hill,
    That looms in grandeur o'er Ardrossan bay!
How bright the beauty of the flashing rill,
    That rushes down the face of Goatfell grey!
How strange that Nature ever can distil
    That liquid thread that never knows decay;
While men in myriads, since its mountain birth,
Have passed for ever from the scenes of earth.

Around are strewn, in ruin'd heaps, the pride
    Of great De Berclay and his lady fair:
Through starlit rooms the bats like spectres glide,
    Where maidens danc'd with jewels in their hair.

The ivy slowly creepeth up the side
    Of walls now ruined, desolate, and bare;
Gone are the warders from De Berclay's towers,
And love and music from his lady's bowers.


Here once they gazed enraptured on the sea,
    And felt delighted with its music grand,
As on its waves came trooping joyously,
    Like merry children, o'er the golden sand.
Now loud, now low its everlasting key
    It sounded to them on the shelly strand—
It still is beautiful—but where are they
Whose songs went sounding o'er the sunlit bay?


Gone to the dusty darkness of the earth,
    Their deeds and generations now unknown!
'Tis sad to see the nettles grace the hearth
    Where love and beauty once had rais'd their throne;
To hear the night winds rave where once reign'd mirth,
    The spacious hall with noxious weeds o'ergrown,
And not a voice to syllable the name
Of those who dreamed once of eternal fame.

## THE CASTLE-HILL.

What's fame or empire, glory or a crown,
    When earth claims all we have, and us at last?
The greatest man's no better than a clown
    When nine or ten decades have o'er him past.
See how the tyrant Time pulls castles down,
    And withers beauty with his blighting blast!
Even robs of letters the memorial stones
That told the virtues of a few great ones.


Contrasted with the ruin at my side
    How fair seems Arran—Queen of Scotia's isles!
The Goatfell, looming in the azure tide,
    Excels the grandest of their lordly piles.
How young and beautiful appears the Clyde,
    On which the setting sun serenely smiles—
Old as creation, yet for ever new,
Each morn presents it to our wondering view.


How bright the sunshine, and how deep the shade,
    That chase each other o'er its fields of blue!
How stately o'er them sweep the teams of trade,
    Yet leave no furrow that the eye can view;

While in their wake, with Union Jack displayed,
    Sail Britain's bulwarks, manned by patriots true—
Our island's safety and our country's pride—
May God go with them o'er the heaving tide.


The radiant sun now sinks on ocean's breast;
    Each flower around me shuts its dewy eye;
In all the beauty of the rainbow drest
    The clouds are glowing in the western sky;
The light haze settles down on Ailsa's crest,
    And stars come trooping o'er the hilltops high;
De Berclay's towers are fading from my view,
I sigh to leave them, but, good night, adieu!

# LADY CATHCART'S LAMENT

Air—"*Jock o' Hazledean.*"

Whaur Lendall glides in sportive pride,
  By Carlton's proud ha',
The Lady sat at evening tide
  Beside the Castle wa';
Sair, sair she grat, for news had come
  That Scotland's king was slain,
An' mony a knight, o' warlike fame,
  Lay cauld on Flodden's plain.

"Oh, will my lord return to me
  And Carrick's peacefu' shore!
Or am I destined wae tae dree
  Alang wi' thousands more?

My brave leal knight, frae Surrey's might
    Would scorn, I ken, to flee;
But if he's slain in Flodden's fight
    I care na when I dee.


"The simmer lichts upon the lea,
    Wi' beauty on its wings,
And o'er each burnie, bush, an' tree
    Unclouded glory flings:
The lav'rock lilts high in the lift,
    The merlin in the grove,
But what is Nature's rarest gift
    Bereft o' Robin's love?


"How dreary Lendall's braes are noo,
    That ance appeared sae fair,
Since he is gane that wont to pu'
    Their flowers to deck my hair!
Amang the broom I lanely mourn
    For him that's far awa',
While in the singing mountain burn
    My tears unheeded fa'."

She raised her head—an' pale he stood,
    In armour, by the stream;
Her cry o' joy rang thro' the wood—
    He vanished like a dream!
When morning came they found her dead,
    Among the waving broom;
Her spirit wi' his wraith had fled
    To Flodden's field o' gloom.

## THE STREAMS.

The streams, the streams, the beautiful streams,
    That sparkle among the trees,
How sweet their song as they dance along
    To the deep unbounded seas!
Where violets grow on shady banks,
    They may a moment stay,
Then swift they rush past brake and bush
    Impatient of delay.
Then sing the streams, the beautiful streams,
    So brilliant, pure, and free,
That seek to rest where the glowing west
    Lights up the azure sea.

The streams, the streams, the bountiful streams,
    That enrich this land of ours,
They kiss the grass as they onward pass,
    And smile on the wildwood flowers:
The lily would pine and the seggan fade,
    The bulrush droop and die,
Were it not the brooks that water the nooks
    Where they hide from the sun's bright eye.
Then sing the streams, the bonny clear streams,
    Whose beauties are free to all;
That flash as pure past the cottage door
    As they do by the lordly hall.

The streams, the streams, the bewitching streams,
    Who has not felt their power
To recall the past, too bright to last,
    Of many a happy hour?
When far away, and the heart is sad,
    We fly, in some sweet dream,
To the cottage door, where we gazed of yore,
    On the singing mountain stream.
Then sing the streams, the silvery streams,
    Whose waters are ever fair;

Time leaves no trace on their sunlit face
    That his fingers were ever there.

The streams, the streams, the enduring streams
    That ever shall remain,
To gladden the earth with their song of mirth
    And rejoice the verdant plain.
Men come and go, but they ever flow
    Undimm'd by circling years,
While we look back on their flowery track
    Oft through the mist of tears.
Then sing the streams, the enduring streams,
    More priceless far than gold,
That ever sweep through the valleys deep,
    Bearing blessings to all untold.

# HOLYROOD.


The morning mist on Arthur's Seat
   Was folding up its garments grey,
And o'er Edina's towers of state
   The sun in golden streams did stray;
As in the palace—Holyrood—
Alone, in silent awe, I stood.

Here Scotland's chivalry, of fame,
   Crown'd and uncrown'd, have stood, like me,
And Queen Victoria—bless her name!—
   Has sat beneath its old rooftree:
Long may her sons and daughters fair
Their royal rule o'er Scotia bear.

The tapestries upon the wall
   Are tatter'd, worn dim by Time;
What stirring mem'ries they recall
   Of hatred, envy, love, and crime!
Here saints have prayed, and captives sighed,
And kings were born, and liv'd, and died.

The Royal portraits seemed to look
   Down on me kind, defiant, brave;
Some as they ill control could brook,
   And others courteous, mild, and grave;
But one fair face among them all
My ardent fancy did enthrall.

It led me captive, back through years,
   To Gallic bowers, of love and song;
And then it changed to sighs and tears,
   And suffered infamy and wrong,
Then pass'd in blood-stain'd clouds away—
*Sic transit gloria,* write I may.

Ill-fated Mary! could no power
   Or guardian angel come between

Thee and the evil-omen'd hour
    Ye wedded Darnley, as a Queen?
Mean, silly coward—Rizzio—
Was foeman worthy such a foe?


Fate ruled it so—the die was cast
    That lost a kingdom and a throne;
The palace of her fathers pass'd
    For ever from her, and alone
She lived to weep—but who has not?—
O'er youthful follies ne'er forgot.


We all are wise when Passion's dead,
    And many faults with others find;
Like sages, how we shake the head,
    And say the world is surely blind,
For in our youth—ah, well-a-day!
I never went but right—astray.


This is the place to moralize
    On human greatness and its end;
I look'd into their stedfast eyes,
    And tried aside the past to rend:

Queen Mary's husband—Darnley—
I scann'd him over many a way.

I look'd at her and then at him,
    But no affinity was there;
His face is senseless, dull, and dim,
    Her's like a seraph's—joyous, fair:
Rare beauty, what a fatal dower
It proves to many to this hour!

It lost a world, some one says,
    The tear in Cleopatra's eye.
Most women have such curious ways,
    That reason's rules they quite defy.
Of this, I'm sure, Queen Mary's face
Would have wrought mischief any place!

And then the bauble called a crown,
    When added to her other charms,
Made chieftains plot, scheme, fight, and frown,
    And keep the country in alarums.
Had Mary been as plain as Bess,
Her nobles would have quarrell'd less:

Though, by the bye, the Tudor dame
    Cost half-a-dozen heads or so ;
Proud Essex tried to fan the flame
    Into a matrimonial glow,
But lost his labour and his head—
The icy virgin would not wed.

Poor Mary's heart was form'd to love
    Mirth, music, sentiment, and song ;
Her cultur'd mind was far above
    The ghostly guides and courtly throng
That flutter ever round a throne
Till sets its sun, and then they're flown.

If youthful follies were her crimes,
    Her heartless, long captivity
Would have atoned for many times
    Without the last barbarity :
The tragic scene at Fotheringay
Is execrated to this day.

I sadly left Queen Mary's rooms,
    And sought the ruined church below ;

And as I wander'd through the tombs,
Methought I heard her wail of woe
O'er blighted hopes and friends untrue,
Till Holyrood was lost to view.

## CAMREGGAN BURN.

Sing sweetly, Camreggan, a song of the past,
Ere life, with the Autumn of years, was o'ercast,
When among the broom bushes ye lull'd me to sleep,
With thy wild mountain music, enchanting and deep.
The grand airy castles I reared by thy stream,
Through years yet they haunt me in many a dream;
Their gateways were golden—their pathways were fame,
But, alas! they were fleeting, and went as they came.

Sing sweetly, Camreggan, of comrades once dear,
Who broke thy deep silence with many a cheer,
As they joyously bounded o'er rock, scaur, and linn,
'Till Killoup's drowsy echoes were woke by their din.
But the brown, heathy Brachill they'll ne'er tread again,
Or gaze on Killochan, the pride of the plain;
Ungather'd the wild flowers by Girvan may grow,
For between them and Girvan the ocean does flow.

Sing slowly, Camreggan, the requiem of those
Who sleep where the citron of India blows;
Afar from the spot that they lov'd first and best,
'Midst a halo of glory for ever they rest;
And I am left lonely their death-dirge to hymn,
Beside thy old castle and loud-roaring linn,
Where the feathery-fring'd fern bends low o'er the wave,
As if they lamented, like me, for the brave.

Though lonely thy braes, yet, Camreggan, ye sing
The glories of Summer—the beauties of Spring;
The fierce storms of Winter ye proudly defy,
And to Autumn ye thunder "my waters ne'er die."
The seasons sweep o'er thee—undimm'd is thy face—
Years seem but to quicken thy fleet mountain race;
Past ages have swept o'er thy waves like a dream,
And left thee as lovely as ever, fair stream.

## SONG OF THE UNEMPLOYED.


June's come wi' bright blossoms to beautify earth,
   And scatter their perfume around cot an' ha';
To chase gloomy shadows wi' music an' mirth,
   Frae ravine an' mountain, frae streamlet an' shaw.

There's joy in the wildwood, why not in the cot?
   Sure Heaven sends plenty to gladden us a';
The wee chirping sparrow by it's no forgot—
   The lily wi' grandeur a monarch micht chaw.

If earth were unfruitful we ne'er wad repine;
   But when it's sae bounteous we look for a share;
If we shake the vintage we should pree the wine:
   Change places wi' us, an' ye'll think it's but fair.

We sow—do we gather? we weave—do we wear?
    We forge, build, an' launch stately ships on the main;
Yet noo we're left standing like doited King Lear,
    When forced by ingratitude, base, frae his hame.

Like Pharaoh's lean cattle, greed prowls o'er the earth,
    Aye feeding the monster on sinew and brain:
He enters the hovel, sits doon on the hearth,
    An' tugs at the heart-strings o' woman an' wean.

We ask not, proud masters, your riches untold,
    But bread for our children wi' tears do we crave;
Oh! dinna pass by like the Levite of old,
    An' leave us to perish in misery's wave.

When danger menaces ye cling to us then;
    Ere lang ye may need us, my certes, tak' heed,
An' dinna look doon wi' disdain on the men
    Wad peril their lives when their country's in need.

What's gi'en to the needy is lent to the Lord,
    His bank never fails, an' His dividend's fair;
Believe in His promise, accept o' His word,
    An' open your hearts an' your hands to the puir.

## SPRING.

On mossy banks the primrose flings
    Its perfume to the breeze;
And bonnie birdies blythely sing
    Amongst the budding trees.
The lambkins frisk on heathy hills—
    The bairns around the door;
And gladsome sing the bounding rills,
    "The reign o' Winter's o'er!"

The laverock greets the early morn
    Wi' ecstacy and praise;
The mavis frae the blooming thorn
    Trills out its love-sick lays.
In rocky glens deep Echo's voice
    Repeats the amorous strain;
And Dryads through the woods rejoice
    That Spring's returned again.

The streamlet tae the ocean glides
    Amidst the joyous thrang;
While fairies wander wi' their brides
    Its leafy shades amang.
The modest violets blushing view
    Their faces in the stream,
Wi' pearly dewdrops on their bro',
    Like amethysts they gleam.


While music reigns in ilka bower,
    And beauty strews the plain,
While Nature on the earth doth shower
    Her bounteous gifts again—
How fares it wi' the eident swarm
    Amidst the factory's din,
Shut out from every soothing charm
    Of mountain, stream, and linn?


Here traders ruthlessly drive o'er
    The youthful and the old,
An' still insanely sigh for more
    To add to wealth untold.

An' still impiously they cry
    For liberty to all;
And yet Jehovah's laws defy,
    And brethren, poor, enthrall.


Seek not for mercy 'midst the strife
    O' competition's ring,
Whaur gold sits arbiter o' life,
    An' reigns the city's king;
Whaur still ascends the waefu' cry
    O' Labour's sons for bread,
While Mammon's minions pass them by,
    And wish the beggars dead.


Oh! could I, like the birdies, hie
    Awa' tae some sweet stream,
Afar frae every tear and sigh
    Wrung forth by greed and steam,
I'd let them wi' their *vapour god*
    O'er golden treasures sing,
And humbly tread the peacefu' road
    Whaur God's bright flowers do spring.

## IN MEMORIAM: LORD CLYDE.

In anguish we bend o'er his grave to-day,
    And lay aside his sacred sword and shield;
Gone is the star that lighted up the way
    To deathless glory on the battle-field.
Oh! could our tears his noble deeds repay,
    An ample tribute would sad Scotia yield.


Long years ago, upon Corunna's strand,
    With ocean in his rear and foes before,
He stood, unknown to fame, for fatherland,
    Till night in mercy fell upon the shore,
And won a wreath from Gaul's invading band
    To decorate the lonely grave of Moore.

And when he saw the island star grow pale,
    That ever flashed with glory on his sight,
He raised his sword amidst the iron hail
    That rained destruction from the Alma's height,
And cried, "Advance! or Russia tells the tale
    They vanquished Britain in this bloody fight."


Then rose his star, so long obscured and dim;
    Each step he trode his fame grew brighter then;
Then rose from Alma's height the glorious hymn
    Of victory won by Scotland's Highlandmen,
As on they rushed, like torrents o'er a linn,
    That leaps majestic down a mountain glen.


His "thin red line" on Balaklava's plain
    Will never be erased from history's page;
Nor how he stemm'd the deluge of "red rain"
    Evoked by Nana Sahib's savage rage:
These are the deeds that ever will remain
    In Britain's memory till the latest age.

Those are the men deserve the world's applause,
    Who know their duty and perform it well:
Despising fame, they struggle in the cause
    For which a Hampden died, a Wallace fell.
A trophied grave, a multitude's huzzas,
    Ne'er nerved the arm of men like Clyde or Tell.


Among the few immortals let him lie
    Who reaped on earth an everlasting fame;
He served his country with a single eye—
    No higher object ever was his aim.
Now brighter, holier beams his star on high,
    Than those who strove to win the world's acclaim.

## A LAY TO SCOTLAND.

How could I say adieu to thee,
    Hame o' my heart, auld Scotland?
And wander lanely o'er the sea,
    Afar frae frien's in Scotland.
Here first I prest earth's verdant sod—
Here first I found love's lichtsome road—
Here first I knelt in prayer to God—
    Thrice hallowed are ye, Scotland.

I lo'e the purple heather bells
    That grace the hills o' Scotland—
The burnies winding down the dells,
    Like siller threads through Scotland.
For as they wander to the sea
They sweetly seem to sing to me
O' happiness and liberty
    In ha' an' cot o' Scotland.

Altho' not wealthy, yet I'm blest
    Wi' health an' food in Scotland;
Could siller lockit in a kist
    Gie mair afar frae Scotland?
Let ithers wander o'er the deep,
And in Australia fortune seek,
I'll bide at hame an' tend my sheep
    Amang the hills o' Scotland.

Adversity may on us fa',
    An' for a time blight Scotland;
An' pale disease upon us ca',
    An' bring down wae on Scotland.
The same may happen o'er the main,
Has dune before, may do again,
Sae e'en for life I'll wear the chain
    That binds me to thee, Scotland.

When bleak December's mists descend
    An' cast their gloom o'er Scotland,
I find a book, and loving friend,
    Within my cot in Scotland.

There's nae Maories round the door,
Wi' hands begrimmed wi' human gore,
But Peace sits smiling on the shore
   O' patriotic Scotland.


Come weal or wae, whate'er betide,
   I'll stand or fa' wi' Scotland;
Of youth the joy—of age the pride—
   My heart's bound up wi' Scotland.
Whaur sunbeams linger in the West,
Beside the friends that loved me best,
Gie me a grave, and let me rest,
   At last in hallowed Scotland.

## TO A ROBIN.


Sweet Robin, thy song ushers in gloomy Winter,
    To blight a' the beauty o' meadow and tree,
An' howl through the forest the requiem dreary
    O' ilka sweet floweret that blooms on the lea.


How can ye be cheery while around ye are lying
    The children o' Simmer in hosts on the plain?
But maybe ye're dreaming o' Springtide returning,
    An' snatching frae Winter their charms back again.


Or are those wild wood-notes your mode o' lamenting
    O'er Summer departed to land ever green;
Your song sounds o' sadness far mair than o' gladness—
    Your voice frae the housetop brings tears to my een.

It tells that the forest is leafless and eerie;
    It tells that ye're houseless, your offspring a' gane;
It tells that o'er mountain, and moorland, and valley,
    Bleak Boreas is marching with Death in his train!

But come to my cabin, I'll gie ye a shelter,
    An' crumbs frae the table ye'll find at the door;
The bairnies will welcome ye, red-breasted robin,
    An' tell o' your visit when men o' threescore.

When Spring comes wi' garlands o' green o'er the ocean,
    Then hie to the forest, ye're uncaged an' free;
And imitate mankind, ungrateful and selfish—
    Forget a' that friendship conferred upon thee.

## WINTER.

Winter's winds are howling
    Through the valleys bare;
Robin through the wildwood
    Wanders in despair;
Soon he'll seek the housetop,
    Or the window-sill,
And make man's acquaintance
    Sore against his will.

Every brook is brawling—
    Every flower is fled;
Every child is asking—
    Is the bright sun dead?
Scarcely o'er the hill-tops
    Peers his golden eye,
Dreary, dark December
    Makes him very shy.

Buttercups and daisies—
   Coronals of May—
Are they gone forever
   From our sight away?
No! these sleeping beauties
   Will awake again,
When Spring comes with sunshine
   Over hill and plain.


How I love the Summer,
   With its fruits and flowers!
How I hate the Winter,
   With its sleety showers!
Frost and snow—its children—
   Sorely try the poor,
As they rush unbidden
   Through the creaking door.


Wretched, hungry children
   Shivering on the street,
Frost delights to fasten
   On their shoeless feet;

Pinch their wasted faces
    Till aloud they cry—
"Oh, in pity help us,
    Christians, or we die!"


Mistletoe and holly
    Soon will grace the hall;
And, in Christian Scotland,
    Christmas should recall
Acts of self-denial—
    Miracles of love,
Done for us by Jesus,
    That we should improve!


Do not, like the Levite,
    Take the other side;
Help the houseless arabs—
    Christ for them has died!
If they're weak and erring,
    Keep this truth in mind,—
God is ever doing
    Good to all mankind.

## IN MEMORIAM: WILLIAM CLARK.

**DIED 12TH FEB., 1867, AGED 26 YEARS.**

"Dust to dust"—lay him gently down,
He will scarcely be missed in the busy town;
Kind to all, unassuming, mild,
He passed through life like a gentle child.

Only the friends who knew him well
Can of his many virtues tell,
Of the love and faith that lit the way
To the cloudless fields of eternal day.

"Ashes to ashes"—how strange, yet true,
That he who was speaking to me and you
The other day, by his father's hearth,
Now sleepeth beneath yon mound of earth.

But as the mould in the grave fell down,
To the ear of Faith came the joyous sound
That Christ would come and his body raise,
To sit on His throne and hymn His praise.

Spring, bring not the cypress here
To cast its shade over one so dear;
But come with the snow-drops, bright as day,
An emblem of him who has passed away.

His heart was pure as the snowy bloom
That they love to shed on the youthful tomb;
Then come in beauty and gently spread
Their snow-white plumes o'er his narrow bed.

# REST.

Oh! for rest, sighs the factory boy,
Where the birds are singing their songs of joy—
Where the stately trees their shadows cast
O'er the mountain stream as it hurries past;
Where a thousand flowers in beauty spring—
Where a thousand birds are on the wing—
Where echo slumbers amidst perfume,
Afar from the city's sin and gloom.

Oh! for rest, the warrior sighs,
But not where the Summer never dies,
But in the depth of the Highland glen
Untrod by the feet of hostile men—

Where in youth he lay on the purple heath,
And dreamt of winning the victor's wreath;
Of the phantom—glory, honour, fame—
But what are they all but a breath—a name!


Oh! for rest, sighs the sailor brave,
Who has long been tossed on the restless wave;
Not in the land where the palm trees fling
Their grateful shade o'er the desert spring;
Not in the islands that gem the seas,
Where perfume wantons on every breeze;
But in the cot where he dreamt of yore
Of the wonders and wealth of a foreign shore.


Oh! for rest, sighs the merchant proud,
Afar from the din of the busy crowd;
Not where they barter, buy, and sell—
Not where they cheat, and know it well,
But in some quiet, secluded place,
That would the wrinkles of care erase;
Some sweet retreat, unknown to care,
But where on earth is it found—ah! where?

## REST.

Oh! for rest, sighs the weary one,
As she stands on the street in rags alone!
Gone are character, virtue, name—
In the grave let her hide her shame;
There, at least, she in peace can lie,
Men will not mock as they pass her by;
Some one, in pity, a tear may shed
O'er her nameless, narrow bed.

Oh! for rest, sighs the Christian old,
In the city above, with the streets of gold—
Where the water of life pure as crystal flows—
Where the tree of life ever blooms and blows:
No light of the sun is needed there,
For the glory of God maketh all things fair!
And Christ doth wipe from each weeping eye
The tears of earth in His home on high.

## DEATH OF COL. BLAIR, OF BLAIRQUHAN.

O'er Inkerman's mountain the dark cloud of battle
   Is rolling along on its murderous way :
Awake from your slumber, or death from the valley
   Will steal o'er your dreams ere the breaking of day.

He dreams of a spot where the heather is blooming,
   Where Girvan bounds joyously on in its pride;
While his lullaby's sung by the loud cannon booming,
   As fiercely they struggle up Inkerman's side.

Now sharp and incessant the musketry rattle,
   The war-cloud has broken, there's death in the air—
" Up, Guards of my country! we'll conquer in battle,
   Or die on this mountain," said brave COL. BLAIR.

As death quickly passed o'er the dark land of Pharoah,
    To teach its proud tyrant that man should be free;
So foes strew'd the course of the conquering hero—
    He swept through their ranks as a storm o'er the sea.

But the Thistle bends low o'er the flower of the nation;
    He sleeps on the field which his valour has won;
Ever bright be his fame as the dawn of creation,
    When first the dark waters reflected the sun.

Brave BLAIR! tho' thou'rt lying on Inkerman gory,
    Engraved on our hearts will thy mem'ry remain;
And thy name be remembered, till Time waxes hoary,
    As first in the battle and last on the plain.

## LOVELY GALLOWAY.

Though far from thee, fair Garliestown,
    In dreams I see thee yet;
Thy waving woods and sunlit bay
    I never can forget;
While memory can recall the charms
    That Nature does display,—
The flowers that spring, the birds that sing,
    Around fair Galloway.

Love lent his rosy hues to gild
    The beauty of the scene,
As o'er the lawn my winsome lass
    Came tripping like a queen:

The vesper hymn, the mavis' song,
    Swept sweetly o'er the bay,
As on her breast, in blissful rest,
    I gazed on Galloway.


Though fair is Carrick's classic coast,
    And dear the banks of Doon,
Where Burns first struck love's sacred lyre,
    To many a deathless tune;
Yet dearer are the flowery dells,
    Through which I once did stray,
And drank delight from beauty's eyes,
    By lovely Galloway.


I sigh not for Arcadian bowers,—
    Could they bestow the bliss,
The hallowed, happy, joyous hours,
    The love, the happiness,
That I have felt thrill through my heart,
    When roaming by the bay,
With peerless Susan at my side,
    By dear old Galloway?

I seek not fame, but happiness,
    I ask not wealth, but bliss;
Capricious Fortune, hear my prayer,
    Deny all else but this :—
Give me, if but a lowly cot,
    By Garliestown's sweet bay;
O let me live, and love, and die,
    Near lovely Galloway!

## LINES ON ARRAN.

GREAT GOATFELL! on thy rugged peaks
    The bright sun loves to linger long,
And fall in glorious golden streaks
    O'er waters famed in Celtic song.
Like thee, for ever I could gaze
    Upon the sweet enchanting scene,
And sing for aye of Arran's braes,
    Of purple heath and spangled green.

The mountain oak, the birch, the broom,
    The blooming thorn, where herds do stray,
All cast afar their sweet perfume
    O'er Brodick's bonny sunlit bay;
Where fishermen at evening rove,
    Fanned by the breeze that wanders free,
And view the mountains that they love,
    Beneath them shining in the sea.

A hundred rills like silver gleam,
    And, singing, run to kiss the bay,
Where lovers fondly sit and dream
    Fair visions, bright as parting day!
While o'er them nods old Goatfell, grey,
    On which the fleecy clouds do rest,
And all that Nature can display
    Is crowded in the glowing west.

Great Temple of the living God!
    Here are Thy works of wonder seen—
The rifted rock, the flowery sod,
    Declare Thy footsteps here have been.
And though dark ages intervene
    Between us and Creation's dawn,
This lovely, sweet, enchanting scene,
    Attests Thy endless love to man.

## AS LOVE DESCENDS.

As love descends, with sovereign powers,
    To bless the lowly hearth—
As Autumn falls in golden showers
    Upon the groaning earth;
So learning rends the misty shroud
    That dims the human mind,
And falls, like sunshine through a cloud,
    With radiance on mankind.

It gives to youth the power to scan
    Great Nature's endless forms;
It sinks the brute, exalts the man,
    Unnumbered are its charms.
It leads to Wisdom's sacred fane,
    Unfolds the book of love;
It makes the path of duty plain,
    That leads to realms above.

The man is poor, however rich
    Or high his pedigree,
That poesy cannot bewitch,
    And deeds of chivalry.
And rich the man, however poor,
    Can sit and talk with kings,
When Winter rudely shakes the door,
    And through the keyhole sings.

Then onward, upward let us rise
    Above the dross of earth,
And, like immortals, set our eyes
    On things of noble birth.
In every man a brother see,
    The helpless aid, defend,
And love will lead to ecstacy
    In worlds that never end!

## THE DANISH FLOWER.

Sweet, gentle Spring, pray, what do ye bring
    On your wings across the sea?
Beautiful flowers and budding bowers
    Are the gifts I bring to thee.

Since last I was here I have roamed, oh dear!
    Where the feathery palm tree springs,
And lay in the shade that the citron made,
    In the land where the bulbul sings.

But I could not come to Albion home
    Without a floweret rare;
So I wandered on o'er the torrid zone,
    Still searching everywhere.

But nothing I found on that sun-scorched ground
   I thought would grace a bower,
So I sallied forth to the frozen north,
   To look for a modest flower.

I touched with my wand bleak Sweden's strand,
   And told King Frost to go ;
Then shed a tear on Denmark dear,
   And dissolved a winter's snow.

When this was done, out came the sun
   To gladden the frozen north,
And a modest thing that might grace a king,
   Like a rose came blushing forth.

The lily white, and the crocus bright,
   And other gifts I bring ;
But this princely flower, from a Danish bower,
   I give to your future King!

## BATTLE OF INKERMAN.

Alas! for the brave who have fallen to-day,
    On Inkerman's rugged height:
From friends and country far away,
    Defending Britain's right.

And alas! for their friends across the sea—
    For soon they will hear the tale,
That the flower of Scotland's chivalry
    On Inkerman lieth pale.

I weep as I gaze on the blood-stained heath,
    Where around like leaves are strewn,
When Autumn, with its blighting breath,
    Has through the forest blown,

The mighty dead that, in the morn,
    To victory led us on,
Regardless of the iron storm,
    And deathless laurels won.

I see brave Blair stretch'd on the field,
    His Guardsmen by his side;
They did their best their chief to shield,
    And, fighting, nobly died.

I see his sire, with silvery hair,
    Afar, as in a dream,
Sit weeping for the pride of Ayr,
    By Girvan's mountain stream.

He leaves the stream and seeks the hall,
    For restless still is woe,
But each object doth his son recall,
    Oh! whither can he go?

To his grave with grief, like thousands more,
    Whose sons are lying here,
Afar from Scotland's heathy shore,
    With the stars to light their bier,

And the turf beneath them for a bed.
    Beside them low we bow,
And weep and gaze on the honour'd dead,
    With the night-dews on their brow.

## A WELCOME TO GARIBALDI.

The greatest Roman's here to-day
   That ever trode our sea-girt Isle,
Though Rome's proud annals can display
   A thousand names upon her file;
Yet Garibaldi sits alone,
An uncrown'd King on Freedom's throne.

True symbol of unselfish love,
   Without historic pedigree,
His mission still has been to prove
   To Europe Truth's supremacy,
And let earth's greatest despots know
Misrule, at last, will lay them low.

Like Cincinnatus, at the plough,
    His country found him in her need,
Without a thought but when and how
    He might uproot the Bourbon weed,
That, like the deadly Upas tree,
Had blighted lovely Italy.

With patriot power he did diffuse
    New life throughout the nation's heart;
Base Bomba trembled to refuse
    When Garibaldi said, "Depart,"
And Naples saw, with joy elate,
The tyrant's palace desolate.

Then rose from earth to heaven the cry
    Of liberty suppressed so long;
Then Freedom's banner waved on high
    O'er dungeons dismal, dark, and strong,
Where patriots in despair had lain
Till Garibaldi broke their chain.

He led them forth from death and gloom
    Into the glorious light of day,

To breathe the citron's rich perfume,
    To wander by the sunlit bay—
Oh! none can tell what joy they felt,
But those that have in bondage dwelt.

For this, thrice welcome art thou here,
    To Scotland's homes, to Scotland's heart:
Our sires bought Freedom far too dear
    For us to value not the part
You played for mankind's rights, as well
As Hampden, Wallace, Bruce, or Tell.

Free Albion would deny the son
    That did not welcome here to-day
The Chief who at Volturno won
    A fame that time shall ne'er decay;
Whose name will be the patriot's cry
Till wars will cease, and despots die.

## AUTUMN.

Sweet is the sang o' the lark in Spring's morning,
    When dewdrops and gowans bespangle the lea;
Rich are the blossoms the hedgerows adorning,
    When Simmer is beaming on hill, heath, and tree.
But dearer is Autumn that crowns earth wi' plenty,
    And robs for our comfort strath, garden, and plain;
Nae fears o' the future he brings to torment ye,
    But shows ye your losses as weel as your gain.

In Spring time Jock's sighing, " I wish I was single,"
    When sowing the corn amidst wind and rain;
In Autumn contented he sits by the ingle,
    And lilts a sweet sang to his guidwife and wean.
Though flowers are faded and keen winds are blowing,
    And Winter approaching wi' storm in its train,
It may blaw its warst, for his cattle are lowing—
    " Kind Autumn has theekit our fodder again."

In Simmer he's watching the glass and the weather;
    And Tam to herd Crummie frae schule's kept at hame;
To get at the corn she would break the best tether,
    Puir collie wi' keeping her frae it's quite lame.
But Autumn comes birling, denouncing restrictions,
    And byeways like highways re-opens again;
Syne proves to the farmer his fears were but fictions,
    Invented by Satan to puzzle the brain.

For seed-time and harvest are promised for ever,
    By earth's Great Creator, who cannot deceive;
Towards us his love ever flows like a river,
    Although we're ungrateful, and whiles disbelieve.
Spring, Summer, Autumn, he sends with their treasure,
    And Winter, that oft brings the poor to the door,—
Oh! pity, soothe, succour, relieve them with pleasure,
    Ye lend to the Lord what you give to the poor.

## THE LILIES OF THE FIELD.

BEHOLD the lilies of the field,
    How passing beautiful they grow!
How rich the vestments bright they wear,
    And yet they neither spin nor sow.
King Solomon, in all his pride,
    Was not arrayed like one of these—
Sweet modest flowers that gem the earth,
    And scatter fragrance on the breeze!

If God so clothe the flowers we tread,
    Which bloom at noon and fade at night,
Whose beauty's like the snow-flake, seen
    But for a moment, dazzling white,
Then lost for ever to the view,
    The moment that it touches earth—
Man, cares he not far more for you,
    The destined heir of heaven by birth?

The fowls that wing the pathless air,
   With plumage shining like the sun,
They have no barns, and yet they feast
   At God's great table, every one.
But man misdoubts th' Almighty's love,
   Sees in to-morrow only care,
While everything beneath, above,
   A more than Father's love declare.


Live for to-day—the present's thine—
   To-morrow who can call his own?
What's needful to thy happiness
   Is to thy heavenly Father known.
From earth your faithless faces raise,
   In confidence to him above,
And see descending on your race
   His everlasting stores of love!

## SONG OF THE COMING YEAR.

Sixty-four is nearly gone,
    To the ages fled before ;
Sixty-five, with joyous tone,
    Singeth loudly at the door—
" Let the hoary dotard go
In his winding-sheet of snow.

" Flowers are sleeping in the earth,
    Birds are silent, trees are bare ;
Dark December loves not mirth,
    Music drives him to despair.
Therefore let the cynic go,
Since he's so intent on woe.

" I will bring you from the north
    Days for curling, keen and cold ;
Call the modest snowdrops forth,
    Crocuses with hues of gold,

## SONG OF THE COMING YEAR.

Dust of March in bushels bring,
And in April sweetly sing.

"I will come in joyous May,
    And repair your sylvan bowers,
Weave a carpet, bright as day,
    With a thousand wildwood flowers;
And in June, with roses red,
Wreathe a garland for your head.

"In July, by mountain streams
    I will lull you o'er to sleep,
Visit you with happy dreams,
    Where the shade is cool and deep;
And to every hill and plain
August send with fruits and grain.

"I'll enrich the bleakest hills
    With my bright September days;
Hang red rowans o'er the rills,
    As they wander on their ways;
Dye the heath a deeper red,
For the shepherd's mountain bed.

"Brown October comes at last,
　All my brilliant leaves to sere ;
Chill November's bitter blast
　Reaps the glories of the year ;
Dark December's short-liv'd day
Drives me to the past away.


"Use the blessings that I bring
　From the courts of endless love ;
I am ever on the wing,
　Every passing hour improve ;
Grasp my moments as they fly,
For, like me, you're born to die."

## A BIRTH-DAY SONG.

December's winds through leafless trees
    The dirge o' Simmer's singing,
But aye there's flowers that mankind please,
    Still here and there upspringing.
A winsome lass, a bonny boy,
    Are gifts that mak' us cheerie;
Lord Eglinton—I wish him joy—
    Has gotten hame a dearie.

His Lady's name, his Lordship's fame,
    Are dear to a' the nation;
Sae Ayrshire proudly welcomes hame
    This gem o' noble station.
May Providence aye shield her head
    Frae every ill and danger;
By mair than me the prayer is said,
    "God bless the little stranger!"

Oh! may her path be strewed wi' flowers,
    Without a thorn amang them;
For giddy youth in pleasure's bowers
    Oft meet those that wad wrang them.
Lang may her smile licht up the ha',
    Dispelling ocht like sadness;
Lang may her voice ring through the shaw,
    Like Simmer's notes o' gladness.

When age o'ertakes her honour'd sire,
    May she be near to tend him;
Anticipating each desire,
    Frae every ill defend him.
And, lastly, may she win the prize—
    Mair precious far than beauty—
A crown unfading in the skies,
    Bestowed for filial duty.

## THANKS FOR THE LIFEBOAT.

THANKS, kind thanks for the lifeboat strong!
Tho' the gift demands a nobler song
Than ever I sung; but at least I can
Pray for a blessing upon the man
Who gave, unasked, from his private store,
Such a gift of love to his native shore.

To aid the suffering is holier far
Than to spread o'er a land the woes of war;
Better to scatter around us joy
Than descend like the angel of death to destroy,
And defile with blood the beauteous earth,
Leave woe in our trail instead of mirth;
Bequeath to a land happy, rich, and fair,
The terrible legacy,—death, despair.

But the "Earl of Carrick" comes to our bay
With a promise of help on a future day;

When the hurricane sweeps along the shore,
And storm-clouds nestle on Ailsa hoar,
And the fisherman, through the blinding spray,
A wreck descrys in the stormy bay.

Then God-speed the lifeboat and all her crew,
As they dash along like the wild sea-mew,
Through the raging surf to the sailor lone,
Who clings to a spar when his ship is gone;
While around him hisses the yawning wave,
Eager to give him "an ocean grave."

We pray not for tempests to test her powers,
But are truly thankful the means are ours
To rescue the helpless, and rob the wave
Of the prey it threatens—the sailor brave;
And bring home in triumph the gift of life
To the helpless child and the weeping wife.

The sun will grow dim and pass away;
The earth like a garment fade, decay;
But such deeds will outlive the glitt'ring stars,
The honour and fame that are won by wars;
Will circle with glory the giver's head,
When earth and sea are for ever fled.

## ANNIE'S HEAVEN AN' MAIR TO ME.

Oh ! to wander wi' my Annie,
    When the sun has kiss'd the west,
Laid him down in golden glory
    On the ocean's azure breast ;
When the moon, in queenly beauty,
    Sheds her radiance o'er the sea,
Wi' my Annie then beside me,
    Earth seems Heaven an' mair to me !

As she murmurs how she lo'es me,
    As I pree her rosy mou,
Wi' my head upon her bosom,
    That's sae loving, kind, an' true ;
As I see the Cupids peeping,
    Half asleep, frae ilka e'e,
Then I rave, like ane demented,
    Annie's Heaven an' mair to me !

Not the painter, wi' his pencil,
    Could create a form sae fair;
Not the fairest flower o' Simmer
    Wi' my Annie can compare;
Not the sweetest bird that warbles
    Love-notes frae the leafy tree,
Is sae rich an' sae bewitching
    As my Annie's voice to me!

When she speaks I seem to listen
    To the music o' the spheres;
When she smiles she sadness chaseth
    To the land o' sighs an' tears.
Take, capricious fortune, frae me
    Rank an' riches, pedigree,
But in pity leave me Annie,
    For she's mair than life to me!

# GREENAN CASTLE.

### A SERMON FROM STONES.

The God of Day cools his burnished brow
    In the Western waters far away ;
So, as he is making his parting bow,
    I'll sit me down by old Greenan grey,
While the bats and swallows in circles fly
Round its tottering gables grim and high.

A milkmaid's song went over the bay,
    With a tone that bestoke a heart at ease ;
The Western breeze up the Doon did stray,
    To sport among the verdant trees ;
The queen of night, from the azure sky,
Look'd down on the sea with a friendly eye.

I thought, as I sat, upon death and life,
   And how men struggle to win a name;
Of the murder and rapine, war and strife
   Created, acquiring warlike fame—
When a voice from old Greenan hoarsely said,
" Men did the same in the ages fled :

" Here chiefs assembled, and wine flowed free,
   Till my rafters rung with their savage mirth;
When forth they sallied, by land and sea,
   Making desolate many a happy hearth;
But you do your work in a quieter way
   In this intelligent, trading day.

" You read your Bibles, but quite forget
   That fraud and injustice are twins of hell;
You go to church, seldom gamble or bet,
   And the way to heaven can glibly tell :
The panther treads soft, and his look is fair,
But he's more to be feared than the grizzly bear.

" If you gain the world and lose your soul,
   You may count the profit; how great the loss?

Yet you generally live, upon the whole,
    As you didn't care a single toss
About futurity, heaven, or hell;
If you're making money you're doing well.

"That time ever flies is ever forgot,
    Till you trembling stand on the voiceless shore,
Then, despairing, you cry for Salvation's boat,
    The waveless sea to carry you o'er;
You disappear, and all is still,
And your friends find your god in a musty till.

"I've seen in my day a butterfly's ball,
    And midges dance on a Summer's eve;
You're not as ephemeral, but that is all
    The mighty difference I can perceive
Between the insect of a day
    And the man who barters his soul away.

"Oh! would you practise what Christ did preach,
    How blest would be the beautiful earth!
His spirit would come and the nations teach,
    And all would know of the second birth;

And the angel Peace chain the demon War
In some dread abyss from the earth afar."

The wind came soughing across the bay,
    And drown'd the voice, so I heard no more ;
But as I returned upon the way
    I pondered its sermon o'er and o'er,
And I thought, though cynical, old, and grey,
There is wisdom in what the old walls say.

## IN MEMORIAM.

[ The following verses, *in memoriam*, were written as a tribute to the noble heroism displayed by CAPT. BLAKENEY, of the ship "John Gray," which foundered in Morant Bay on January 8, 1868.]


The year is young, but sad the list and long
    Of homes made desolate by thee, O Sea!
How many in thy waters sleep unsung,
    Who sixty-seven hailed with hearty glee,
    As homeward swift they bounded joyously.


Insatiate Sea! why rob us of the brave,
    And spare the coward trembling on through years?
How wierdly wild the requiem ye do rave
    Of those whose heroism claim our tears—
    And BLAKENEY'S name in thy sad list appears.

"The storm," he said, " sweeps fiercely o'er the sea,
    The Lizard Point we cannot round to-night;
The treacherous shore is close upon our lee,
    Like winding-sheets I see the breakers white:
    Let's drop the anchor till to-morrow's light."

The anchor's dropp'd, but onward still she bounds,
    Like an impatient courser, through the gloom:
More near, more clear, more fearful grow the sounds
    Of breakers roaring, as she nears her doom—
    "Prepare, brave BLAKENEY, for a watery tomb!"

Like Martin, of the "London," firm he stood,
    And waved the signal light, for aid, on high;
He saw the lifeboat breast the seething flood;
    He saw his crew depart, but scorn'd to fly,
    Preferring rather at his post to die.

Young, fearless even to a fault, and brave,
    He knew his duty and performed it well—
Too well, alas! or else the seething wave
    Would ne'er have borne him lifeless on its swell,
    And left friends weeping as his fate they tell.

Had noble daring saved him from the wave,
    He might have fearless braved the fiercest gale;
His was the intrepidity which often saves
    A ship and crew where good men even fail,
    And for a moment hesitate and quail.

Peace to his ashes, by the sounding sea;
    Peace to his spirit, in the haven of love;
Peace to the friends that sorrow's cup must dree;
    Peace give them, Father, till they meet above,
    And o'er its blissful plains for ever rove.

## BROUNSTONE CASTLE.

Oh, to stray by Brounstone Castle,
    When the shades of evening fall!
When the moonbeams glide in glory
    Through the baron's ancient hall.
Oh, to hear the Girvan singing,
    As it sung langsyne to me!
When beside me sat my Annie
    Underneath the trysting tree.

Ask the winds that ever wander
    Through the ruined starlit hall;
Ask the flowers that bloom in beauty
    By the hoary, ivied wall—
Did they e'er behold a lady
    Tread the hall, on festive night,
With a step as light as Annie's,
    With an eye so black and bright?

## BROUNSTONE CASTLE.

All the bloom that heralds Summer
    With her face can ne'er compare;
All the plumage of the raven
    Is outrivall'd by her hair.
Like the snowdrop, pure and spotless,
    Nodding in the sunbeams bright,
Is her brow—and, oh! her bosom
    Makes me dizzy with delight.

Gone are minstrel, knight, and lady,
    From the Castle and its bowers,
But around my heart will ever
    Linger mem'ries of the hours
That I spent with peerless Annie,
    By the Girvan's mountain stream:
Time will never dim the beauty
    Of that happy, short-lived dream.

## CRUGGLETON CASTLE.

### A REMINISCENCE.

Cruggleton, beneath thy archway,
    Leaning o'er the restless sea,
Have I sat beside a maiden
    Fairer, dearer far to me
Than the azure of the ocean,
    Than the fragrant clover lea,
Than ambition, fame, or glory,
    Or ancestral pedigree!

Cruggleton, beneath thy archway
    I may never rest again;
But in nightly dreams I see thee
    Bending o'er the heaving main,
With that peerless maid beside thee,
    Shedding beauty o'er decay,
Chasing shadows from thy ruins
    With her smile, as bright as day.

## CRUGGLETON CASTLE.

Cruggleton, the flowers of Summer
   Wreath thy tempest-beaten head,
But the one that crowned thy beauty
   Is for ever from thee fled !
Idly they may bloom and wither
   On thy summit, old and grey,
Since the fairy form has vanished
   That transformed thy gloom to day!

Cruggleton, the storms of Winter
   Some wild night may lay thee low,
Hurl thy lone and hoary archway
   To the dread abyss below;
But eternity will never
   That fair maiden's form efface—
All the love and all the beauty
   Beaming from her sunny face !

## ARDROSSAN CASTLE.

Richardus de Berclay, though great was thy Castle—
    Though great was thy prowess and wide-spread thy fame,
Thou'rt now as unknown as thy henchman or vassal
    That sleeps by thy side in the grave's dark domain.

From turret to donjon its ruins are lying;
    The voices are silent that gladdened the hall;
The winds thro' the rents made by Time now are sighing,
    And ivy is feasting upon the grey wall.

No more from the towers the banners are streaming,
    O'er chiefs going forth to the hunt or foray;
No more in its bowers fair ladies are dreaming
    Of knights winning glory on fields far away.

The stars light the chambers where minstrels have chanted
    The deeds done in battle our country to free;
But now they are desolate, roofless, and haunted,
    By wandering winds from the western sea.


They roam through the rooms, and for ever they're sighing,
    O'er beauty departed and valour that's gone ;
For low in the dust knight and lady are lying,
    And ruin sits gnawing the Castle alone.


Destroying, restoring, and changing for ever,
    Time raised up Ardrossan to beautify Clyde—
Oh! may its sweet villas in ruins lie never,
    But still look as fair as its guardian tide.

## LINES ON THE MARRIAGE OF A DEAR FRIEND.

Could I, like Summer, on the earth,
    Strew flowers upon your youthful way,
Or weave a rosy blooming bower
    Where sunbeams linger all the day,
For her and thee I'd make a home
    In some sweet flowery solitude,
Where love would dwell amidst perfume,
    And carking care would ne'er intrude.

But this I can do—wish to her
    And thee content, peace, joy, and health;
The first is more than pedigree,
    The rest are never bound to wealth;
Or if they had, your servant's share
    Of worldly comfort would be small;
But Heaven's impartial in its ways,
    And showers its blessings down on all.

God bless your union! may your lives
    Run sweetly as a flowery stream,
Until you reach the waveless sea
    Where ends the glory of life's dream.
Then may Christ at the narrow gate
    Receive you in His gracious arms,
And take you forth to nightless fields,
    Begemm'd with Heaven's eternal charms.

## THE HARVEST MOON IS STREAMING, LOVE.

The harvest moon is streaming, love,
    Like silver o'er the sea;
The radiant stars are beaming, love,
    Upon the dewy lea:
Then meet me by De Berclay's tower,
    Upon the Castle Hill,
And we will drink, if but an hour,
    Of love, as from a rill.

The azure waves are singing, love,
    Their music to the moon;
The fragrant flowers are flinging, love,
    Their perfume to the tune;
The bats are at their evening ball
    Among the ruins grey:
Then meet me by the ivied wall,
    And hear what love can say.

A loving heart's my tocher, love,
    And that is truly thine :
I'd give the gold of Ophir, love,
    To say that yours was mine ;—
To fold you in my arms to-night,
    So beautiful and still,
Among the pearly dewdrops bright,
    Upon the Castle Hill.

My heart is weary waiting, love,
    For wealth that ne'er will come ;
The birds when they are mating, love,
    Take love to bless their home.
Then meet me on the Castle Hill,
    Among the ruins grey,
And drops of nectar we'll distil,
    To drink some future day.

## LINES ON THE DEATH OF A YOUNG LADY.

Gone home! and left a world of care,
  To lands of sweet, seraphic bliss:
The flower we lov'd was far too fair
  To blossom in a spot like this;
Where death, disease, and sorrow fling
Their shadow o'er the fairest thing.

Gone home! and left us mourners here
  To scatter flowers upon her grave;
And through the mist of many a tear
  Behold the form to earth we gave—
For memory and affection still
Recall the truly lov'd at will.

## LINES ON THE DEATH OF A YOUNG LADY.

Gone home to Jesus! and the host
    Who sing the glories of his grace;
Safe landed on bright Canaan's coast,
    With Abraham's angelic race,
Through coming ages evermore
To worship, praise, and Christ adore.

Gone home to heaven! we'll grieve no more,
    But imitate her virtues rare;
And meet her on the happy shore,
    Where all is blissful, endless, fair—
And every tear is wiped away,
That dims the mourner's eye to-day.

## THE BONNY STREAMS O' AYRSHIRE.

The bonny Streams o' Ayrshire,
    As on their course they run,
Like siller belts around the hills
    They sparkle in the sun.
And Simmer spreads the fairest flowers
    Upon their classic braes,
Whaur linger still the echoes sweet
    O' Burns's deathless lays.

The beauties o' the Doon and Ayr
    Are sung in mony a land,
Whaur music floats through myrtle bowers,
    Far frae famed Carrick's strand;
But Girvan hides its unsung worth
    Amongst its leafy shaws,
And jinks an' jouks by broomy knowes,
    And ancient lordly ha's.

There let me stray an hour or sae
    Upon its braes, and dream,
Whaur fair Killochan's stately trees
    Are mirrored in the stream.
Oh, haunts o' youth! oh, hame o' love!
    Yet through the mist o' years
They rush unbidden on my sicht,
    An' blin' my e'en wi' tears.

The world has only left me this—
    The memory o' the past;
It canna take what Time has spared
    Unclouded to the last.
The fairy stream, the flowery dells,
    Dear, though unkent to fame—
The hallowed haunts, for ever fair,
    Around my youthfu' hame.

## BEAUTIFUL MAY.

Vocal as ever with music and mirth,
May has returned to beautify earth :
Joyously tripping o'er moorland and green,
Scattering gifts like a bountiful queen ;
Breathing her fragrance through wildwood and dell,
Shedding rich sunshine on mountain and fell ;
How the green hedgerows their rich robes display,
Fresh from the fingers of beautiful May.

Shaking the bright dews of earth from his wings,
The lav'rock with ecstacy heavenward springs ;
Over the streamlet the swallow does skim,
Trying to twitter, like others, a hymn.
Humming and working, the bees are abroad,
Where the bright blossoms in myriads nod ;
Meadows appear like the sky's milky way,
Garnished with gowans by beautiful May.

Into the ravine the sun sends his beams,
Drying the beds of the dark mountain streams;
Making the waters that none dared to ford,
Shallow and bright as a silvery cord.
Over the crag now the wild flowers creep,
Where lately the dark troubled waters did sweep;
Lowly the cataract now seems to say—
"Thrice are ye welcome back, beautiful May!"

Come from the city and share the soft breeze,
Sighing and dying among the green trees;
Sweet is the music that rings through the grove,
Breathing of harmony, innocence, love.
Come to the shade of the fern-fringed rock,
Where the lone shepherd is tending his flock;
And sadness will flee from your heart far away,
When breathing the incense of beautiful May!

## DREAM OF THE LITTLE COTTON-PIECER.

In dreams I strayed where wavelets played,
  And zephyrs wandered free;
Where the sun went down like a golden crown
  On the brow of the azure sea.

The spirits of air were rejoicing there,
  On cloudlets white as snow;
With sunbeams drest far in the west,
  They sported to and fro.

On uplands green, beside the stream,
  The browsing herds did stray;
From wildrose bush the happy thrush
  Did trill his joyous lay.

O'er rocks sublime the heath and thyme
  Did hang in festoons gay;
While, lone, afar the evening star
  Peeped o'er their summits grey.

Here, truly blest, I sank to rest
    Beside the rushing linn—
Far from the strife of city life,
    Its foppery, rags, and sin.

Where the sun at noon looks like the moon,
    Seen through the haze of night;
Where want and woe like spectres go,
    The heart and home to blight.

Where fierce disease feeds at his ease
    Upon the famished poor;
While wealth and pride superbly glide
    In phaetons by their door;

Where traders meet to goad and cheat
    Such wretched things as I,
Who but in dreams can stray by streams
    Beneath the Summer sky.

While they can stray o'er landscapes gay,
    Where I would gladly roam,
They say the breeze from Western seas
    Might save me from the tomb.

How long, O God! shall wealth, roughshod,
    Ride over children dear?
And see them sigh, pine, sicken, die—
    But vengeance may be near.


God's chosen band in Egypt's land
    Did long in bondage groan;
He made the waves rescue the slaves,
    Triumphant and alone.

# PEACE, COLUMBIA!

Stern Confederates and Federals
  Do forego your savage strife;
Listen to the voice of Mercy,
  Crying, "Spare a brother's life!"

See your halls and huts deserted,
  See your fair fields drench'd with gore;
See your wives and mothers weeping;
  Ground your muskets—fight no more.

War's a game that leads to ruin;
  War's unholy, therefore pause;
If the South have erred, forgive them;
  That's the way to gain applause.

Sweeter far the voice of conscience
    Whispering ye have acted right,
Than the proudest trophy wrested
    From an enemy in fight.

Can ye, in the name of Freedom,
    Seek a brother to enthral?
If ye could, would, did enslave him,
    That's not liberty at all.

Liberty's unsullied banner
    May be lost, but never won,
By the acts of foul aggression
    Which insensate men have done.

Can ye subjugate a nation
    That's determined to be free?
As well try, with swords and muskets,
    To obstruct the swelling sea.

Why destroy a land of beauty
    With the hell-hounds bred by war?
Dabble in each other's life-stream
    Fair Columbia's glittering star?

Listen now to sober reason,
 Pleading thus with earnest voice—
" Yankees, cease this wicked warfare,
 Let the nation's heart rejoice!"

See Columbia's mothers kneeling
 By their offsprings' gory biers;
Listen now to Mercy pleading—
 Ground your muskets, dry those tears!

## THE EMIGRANT'S FAREWELL.

Farewell to the Binehill and Saughhill for ever,
　Sweet valley of Girvan, for ever adieu!
While memory remains will I doat on thy river,
　Where oft I hae wandered wi' friends kind and true.
A hame and kind friends I may find o'er the ocean,
　And want and its woes keep afar frae my door;
But still to the West will I turn with devotion,
　And sigh for the beauties of fair Carrick's shore.

Penkill and Pinwhauple, Killochan, Old Dailly—
　Oh, dear are their deep glens and wildwoods to me!
When I gaze on their grandeur my heart's like to fail me;
　'Tis want drives me from them across the deep sea.
Oh, blest is the fleet roe can bound thro' the greenwood;
　Oh, happy the laverock can dwell on the lea,
Beside thee, Killochan, loved haunt of my boyhood,
　And hame of my heart when I'm far o'er the sea.

The roses of June round the woodbine are twining,
    And nodding in beauty above Girvan's stream;
The last beams of day on its waters are shining,
    Ere they fade from my sight like a beautiful dream.
The brow of the Saughhill is gilded wi' glory;
    But ere the sun gladdens its grey peaks again,
And looks on lone Ailsa, majestic and hoary,
    I will be afar frae my kindred and hame.

## SONG OF THE CARRICK FISHERMAN.

My boat rocks in the Maiden's bay,
    And frae my cottage door
I see the wavelets gently play
    Upon the sunlit shore.

Culzean's grey towers, wi' lordly pride,
    Cast shadows o'er the sea,
O'er which my bonny bark doth ride
    Wi' bounding, reckless glee.

Though dear to me are Carrick's hills,
    Its flowery nooks and dells,
Sweet verdant slopes an' silver rills,
    An' blooming heather bells;

Yet dearer are the azure waves,
    The guardians o' my hame;
The wind in freedom o'er them raves,—
    Sports with their snowy mane.

## SONG OF THE CARRICK FISHERMAN.

When morning wi' its rosy blush
    Sweeps darkness frae the sky,
We o'er the waters gladly rush,
    My bonny boat and I.

And when day sinks upon their breast,
    We steer for Carrick's shore ;
The golden stream flung frae the West,
    Lichts, leads us tae the door.

The ha' of Bruce in ruin lies—
    The ocean's still the same ;
It wears a youth that Time defies,
    And leads to wealth and fame.

On it Britannia's sun arose,
    And ever seems to smile
Upon the daring sons of those
    Who conquered at the Nile.

## THE SABBATH.

Hail! peaceful, holy day of rest!
Unto the weary doubly blest;
Could I, like Graham, thy glories sing,
And all the blessings thou dost bring,
For ever would I chant thy praise
In his endearing, deathless lays.

Blest day! to man in mercy given
By ever kind, indulgent Heaven,
To lift us far above the care
That here besets us every where,
To lands where grace and glory flow,
And joy supplants the place of woe.

Thrice hallowed day, with peace it comes,
To cheer the highest, lowest homes;
To shut out darkness, let in light,
Point out the wrong and show the right,

From the Eternal Word of Truth—
The stay of age, the guide of youth.

None dare command us on that day
To work—I'm wrong, forgive me pray—
Some do command, should we obey,
And desecrate the sacred day?
If gold's their god, then let them kneel
And turn that day his glittering wheel.

When God had called this lovely earth
From darkness, chaos—wondrous birth!
Through space the planets made to roll,
And given man a deathless soul,
He rested on the seventh day,
But hear what some to that do say:

"Sir, I'm a Christian, not a Jew,
Know right and wrong as well as you;
Our quaint forefathers knew no better
Than follow Scripture to the letter,
But I know something more than heed
Their Jewish jargon, canting creed.

"On Sunday, Sir, I take the air,
By rail or boat—no matter where—
And listen to the babbling brooks;
Seek out the cool, sequestered nooks,
Where ferns fringe the roaring linn,
Afar from city life and sin.

"Friend citizen, you're free to go
Where streamlets murmur, flowers grow,
But when you choose to take the air,
Drive ever your own coach and pair:
In everything ye think or do,
Act like a Christian, not a Jew."

## ON HEARING A MAVIS SING IN GLASGOW.

Sing on, sweet bird, your joyous notes
    To labour's sons proclaim,
As on the breeze their music floats,
    That Winter's ceased to reign.
That Spring has come with vernal showers,
    Tae busk fair Scotia's braes,
An' 's thrang at wark, in sylvan bowers,
    Preparing Simmer's claes.

'Tis rare to hear a captive sing
    Sae sweet and joyously,
But sweeter far thy notes would ring
    Frae some auld hazel tree;
By wimpling burn or mountain glen,
    I there might join your strain,
But in this crowded mart of men
    I try to sing in vain.

My spirit wi' thy song is borne
    Whaur uncag'd warblers dwell ;
Whaur music bursts frae whin an' thorn
    In mony a flowery dell.
By Girvan's sweet secluded stream,
    Around Kilkerran's ha ;
When violets close their glistening e'en,
    In dreams I'm wi' them a'.

Oh, would propitious fortune smile
    Upon my humble lot,
I'd hie me to the green woods wild
    Around my native cot.
There Mammon never forged the chain
    That fetters thee an' me :
Then sing again thy cheerfu' strain,
    It sounds o' liberty.

## A FAREWELL.

Sweet home of my childhood—bright land of the West!
Where the stars light the ocean when day goes to rest—
There is no spot on earth that to me seems as fair,
For the daydreams of glory were first woven there.

There oft have I wander'd by Girvan's sweet stream,
While Summer and sunshine enlivened the scene,
And wove in my fancy those visions sublime,
Which are now cast like wrecks on the ocean of Time.

How saddening to think that the world's weary care
Should bend its dark shade over visions so fair,
And bury the beauty of youth's hopeful dream,
Beneath the dark waters of life's turbid stream.

The world may deceive, trusted friends turn cold,
But the heart's first affections they never grow old;
Like springs in life's desert that gladden the heart,
They cling to us fondly when all else depart.

Though my name be effaced in that bright sunny land,
Erased like the footprints I left on its sand,
Yet my heart fondly clings to its wave-beaten shore,
And I yet love the spot where I sported of yore.

Then give me a grave in the land of the West,
Beside the loved parents my childhood caressed:
Oh! lay me at last near the echoing waves,
Where the sun's parting glory will rest on our graves.

## ARDMILLAN BAY.

When South winds howl round Ailsa's peaks,
    An' Arran's wreathed wi' snaw,
When dowie birdies cower their wings
    In ilka leafless shaw :
When low has sunk the Wintry sun
    Behind the Bennan grey,
There's shelter for the gallant bark
    In fair Ardmillan Bay.

Majestic mountains, wild and grand,
    Loom o'er its azure tide ;
While at their base the stately ha'
    Looks o'er the spreading Clyde.
The fisherman, the sailor brave,
    Ha'e blest the friendly ray
It sends, at nicht, across the waves,
    To cheer their pathless way.

I've sported wi' the tiny waves
    That o'er the sand did stray,

When Simmer wreathed wi' thyme the rocks
    To hide their faces grey.
Frae Woodlands bank the blackbird's notes
    Were wafted o'er the sea;
While o'er the bay the bonny boats
    Went bounding merrily.

I've watched the cloudlets in the West
    Their brilliant hues unfold,
When parting day prest Ocean's brow
    An' tipt his waves wi' gold.
Then dreamed these might be palaces
    Where airy sprites did play,
In gorgeous sunbeams richly drest,
    That floated far away.

Oh! could the weary find a spot
    Like this, so passing fair,
Life's e'ening sun would never set
    Enveloped in despair!
But hope would spring within their hearts,
    Diffusing joyous rays;
As flowers in Summer fragrance shed
    Upon Ardmillan braes.

# GLENDOUNE.

The Western waves are hushed to rest
    On Ardwell's thyme-wreathed rocky shore;
The Seagulls seek their lofty nest
    Amongst the crags o' Ailsa hoar:
A' Nature's hushed, unless the rill
    That babbles to the rising moon,
That's peering ower the great Saughhill,
    Upon the lands o' fair Glendoune.

An' never on a fairer scene
    Did Luna gaze wi' placid e'e;
The gowans sparkle on the green,
    The stars upon the sleeping sea.
Oh! could I sing, like bards o' yore,
    Auld Coila's harp I would attune,
And sound aloud o'er Scotia's shore
    The peerless beauties o' Glendoune.

Oft ha'e I climbed its mountain steep,
    An' felt my heart dilate wi' pride,
As ower the waves my eye did sweep
    To Arran's hills beyond the Clyde—
Whaur Ossian, frae his cloudy car,
    Yet to its children seems to croon,
How chieftains led their clans to war,
    To guard sic lands as thine, Glendoune.

Lang years have fled since first I prest
    The blooming heathbells on its brae,
And watched the bright sun sink to rest
    Behind the peaks o' Arran grey;
But still its face, like ocean's waves,
    Is fresh and bright as rosy June;
An' still I dream through Ardwell's caves
    Resound the glories o' Glendoune.

## A WINTER STORM.

With frigid breath comes Winter bleak
    Upon his dark career,
Thro' leafless woods to howl and shriek
    The requiem of the year.

From snowy Lapland, vast and drear,
    He comes with icy chain,
To bind the lakes and fountains clear
    Within his cold domain.

Now scarcely peeping o'er the hills,
    The sun looks on the scene;
The leaves lie dead on frozen rills,
    Gone is their Summer green.

No more are heard the wildwood lays
    That hailed his rising beam;
No more he sheds his cheering rays
    On mountain, moor, and stream.

Slow flies the home-returning crows,
    Confused and low their flight,
As if a host of airy foes
    Arose upon their sight.

In fitful gusts the wind doth moan
    And rave around the door;
God help the shepherd out alone
    This night upon the moor.

The lonely mother hears the blast
    Around her cottage roar,
And sees her son cling to the mast,
    Far from the friendly shore.

The seething waves around him foam,
    Impatient for their prey,
"If lost, then desolate is my home!"
    She cries in dread dismay.

Now charity treads the dingy street,
    Where misery's glad to hide;
Regardless of the drenching sleet,
    She seeks the lone bedside.

Samaritan-like, she acts her part,
  Gives largely of her own,
And feels a joy within her heart
  To avarice never known.

If Heaven has given wealth and power,
  Improve the gifts to-day,
For life, alas! is like the flower
  That's doomed to fade away.

The leaf that falls in the mountain stream,
  From the autumn-stricken tree,
And passeth away like a sleeper's dream,
  Is an emblem, Man, of thee.

The Summer saw it bud and bloom
  Beneath its sunny eye;
The Autumn winds prepared its tomb,
  And Winter saw it die.

## LINES SUGGESTED BY THE ARRIVAL OF LORD CLYDE.

With heartfelt joy and Scottish pride
    We welcome back again
The noble soldier, brave Lord Clyde,
    From India's battle plain;
Adorned with laurels nobly won
From Bramah's " Children of the Sun."


In distant graves the strongest sleep
    Since last he trode this shore;
Brave Neill lies by the Jumna deep,
    And Havelock near Cawnpore;
But deathless glory crowns the band
Who fought and fell for fatherland.

## LINES SUGGESTED BY THE ARRIVAL OF LORD CLYDE.

Within the nation's loving heart
    Their names will find a place,
Nor from that vital seat depart,
    While live the Saxon race—
To guard the fame, the hallow'd graves,
Of those who lie beyond the waves.

But Colin claims the highest meed
    Of British minstrel's lays,
From stately Thames to silvery Tweed
    Let's sing the warrior's praise,
Who stemmed the fierce, red, bloody tide
That cruel Siva ruled with pride.

Then Nana Sahib fled before
    The sword ne'er drawn in vain,
As many live who yet deplore
    Its gallant use in Spain;
And on Crimea's deadly field
It fought to conquer—ne'er to yield.

And there he formed the "thin red line"
    On Balaklava's plain,

And with a bravery rare to find
    Did Russia's hordes restrain,
And taught the foe to *know* the band
The Scottish chieftain did command.

Thou mighty conqueror of the East,
    Britannia writes thy name,
And though the last, yet not the least,
    In her bright roll of fame,
And on its page thy deeds will glow,
While lives the mem'ry of Lucknow!

# ON THE DEATH OF THE REV. WILLIAM DILL, COLMONELL.

Could learning, piety, or worth,
    Have saved a pastor, loved so dear,
Beside his grave I ne'er had stood,
    Nor shed the sympathetic tear
    O'er one so good, so kind, sincere.

'Tis hard to think his loving heart
    Is silent as the earth I tread;
His smiling face I oft recall,
    And wonder if he can be dead,
    With throbbing heart and aching head.

But this sad stone proclaims the tale,
    His form is hastening to decay;
I hear the winds around it moan;
    The good, the kind has passed away,
    And we are spared another day.

No more I'll hear his voice proclaim
    The glorious gospel's loving theme ;
No more I'll see him stray at eve
    By Stinchar's sweet, pellucid stream,
    On heavenly themes to muse and dream.

No more I'll see his children fair
    Around him gathering to hear
The wondrous tale that moved to mirth,
    Or made them sigh and drop a tear:
    Alone they're left in sorrow here.

But all the precepts that he taught
    They will remember evermore,
Until they meet, no more to part,
    Their father on that happy shore,
    To worship God for evermore.

## BRITAIN'S VOLUNTEERS.

Vain Gauls may boast of coming o'er
    To conquer Britain's isle;
But let them land upon its shore,
    We'll meet them with a smile;
Nor part, though death in frightful forms
    Upon the field appears,
Until each braggart grounds his arms
    To Britain's Volunteers.

For never shall a foeman tread
    Upon the hallow'd graves
Where sleep the honour'd, mighty dead,
    Who nobly ruled the waves.
Look back on Spain's red battle-field,
    And proudly there appears
A proof they'd rather die than yield—
    The British Volunteers.

The pathway to Victoria's throne
    Lies through the Nation's heart—
Ere there a Gallic trumpet's blown
    It's life-stream must depart;
And buried be the chivalry
    Our ancient land reveres,
When foemen meet in revelry
    O'er conquered Volunteers.

If e'er they cross our guardian waves,
    We'll set their spirits free;
We gave unto their fathers graves
    Upon the land and sea;
And, British valour still the same,
    No foreign foeman fears,
Nor that a despot can enchain
    True British Volunteers.

## A CHRISTMAS CAROL.

Hail! Christmas, with thy sunny tide
   Of rare old memories dear!
We welcome thee with joyous pride,
   And reverence most sincere.
Thy mission is to cheer the heart,
And reunite friends long apart.

The hoary head—the lisping tongue—
   With gladness greet the day
On which angelic minstrels sung
   This sweet seraphic lay—
" Good-will and peace to all we bring,
From Heaven's ever gracious King."

To love and friendship give the rein
   Of life's impatient steed;
And let us for a day detain
   On pleasure's flowery mead.

Come, sing the good old songs to-night;
*Langsyne* gives rapturous delight.

Bring forth the heroes of the past
   From Time's obscuring gloom,
Who crushed Imperial legions vast,
   And fighting found a tomb.
And youth will learn how Britons can
E'en win such fields as Inkerman.

Let those beware beyond the sea,
   Who think that spirit's fled;
We wish to live in amity,
   But, by the mighty dead,
If foemen dare to cross the waves,
On freedom's soil we'll give them graves.

When mnsic fills the lighted hall
   That youth and beauty tread;
'Tis then the memory will recall
   The dear departed dead,
And drop the tribute of a tear
To Ayrshire's chief—Montgomery dear.

The fairest, bravest, for him mourn,
   Why not the humble poor?
He never heard their plaint with scorn,
   Nor shunned the widow's door:
But in his Son again we see
His noble liberality.

Insatiate year! could'st thou not go
   In mercy by the throne?
Another Princely Head laid low!
   Thou'rt surely weary grown
Of casting on the earth thy blight—
Of clouding homes that else were bright.

But life's a dream, and death's a sleep
   Reserved alike for all:
We part in grief—in joy we meet
   Where no dark shadows fall:
So let us sing, at least to-day,
A merry Christmas roundelay.

## THE SUN'S GANE TO REST.

The sun's gane to rest, love, behind yon great mountain,
    That looms in wild grandeur across the deep sea;
The stars beam in beauty upon the clear fountain,
    The gowans are sleeping upon the green lea.
The voices are mute o' the birds in the wildwood;
    The bat, like the swallow, now winnows the air;
O come to the burn whaur we paidled in childhood;
    Like thy bonny sel', Jean, it's face is aye fair.

The wild rose nods there, to the bright water singing,
    Awa' to its hame in the wide-spreading sea;
While o'er it the woodbine its fragrance is flinging,
    And hushed is the hum o' the wild mountain bee.
Years, lang years ha'e fled since we pu'd the red heather,
    To theek the wee houses we bigg'd on its braes;
An' wove 'neath the hazel, our wee heads thegither,
    Those visions as bright as the sun's setting rays.

When far, far awa', love, I ever was dreaming
    Upon the fair face that I loved mair than fame;
It cheer'd me whaur war's gory banner was streaming,
    Afar frae my country, my kindred, an' hame.
Afar frae this burnie, its heath-bells, an' gowans,
    I dream'd o' my Jeanie across the deep sea;
I dream'd o' the spot whaur we pu'd the red rowans,
    An' shook the brown nits frae the auld hazel tree.

Sweet haunts, ever dear, whaur in life's sunny morning
    We followed the minnows that play'd in the stream;
While o'er us the midges their dances were forming,
    Whaur we danc'd like them on the daisy-clad green.
Here, blest wi' your love, in the lowliest sheiling,
    The sun o' enjoyment wad ne'er set again:
She sunk on his bosom—her blushes concealing—
    An' murmured, "Dear laddie, my heart's a' yer ain."

## SONG OF THE SHUTTLE.

While before the surge retreating
    Of great Mammon's swelling wave,
Still the shuttle keeps repeating
    "Death will liberate the slave."

As the Summer crowns with glory
    Every flower that decks the land,
So the shuttle's ancient story
    Makes the fairest look more grand.

If the fair, their skill's arraying,
    Only knew how hard's their fate,
Soon the ladies would be laying
    Some good plan to help their state.

From the first who ruled in Eden,
    To the one who rules at home,
Busy wife or blushing maiden,
    Wield a power the greatest own.

## SONG OF THE SHUTTLE.

Summer comes—they feel the sunshine
   Through the plate-glass overhead;
But the clover or the woodbine
   Ne'er for them their fragrance shed.

All the flowers they see are woven
   'Midst the factory's dust and din,
Where the few by fortune chosen
   *Lock them out and lock them in.*

They can stray by glen or mountain;
   With their children seek the shore;
Sit beside the coolest fountain
   Till the noonday's heat is o'er.

Buy their daughter sweetest music,
   For her boudoir all things fine;
And to catch the lordly Spendquick,
   Silk, brocade, and crinoline.

But the weavers' little children,
   They can never get new clothes;
How they live is quite bewildering,
   Yet they're happy quite as those

Who chicane, and cheat, and grovel,
 For the gold that rules the town;
Who invade and rob the hovel,
 Pinch the poor, and keep them down.

If they shake for you the vintage,
 Let them taste the ruby wine:
Give to labour fair per centage,
 And they'll take it very kind.

## OH! DINNA LEAVE FAIR SCOTIA'S SHORE.

Oh! dinna leave fair Scotia's shore
   In search o' wealth and fame;
Wi' cheerfulness your lot I'll share,
   But, Jamie, bide at hame.
For a' the wealth Australia boasts,
   Bestowed on me this day,
I wadna leave the flowery dells
   Whaur we in youth did stray.

They may be fair those distant climes,
   Whaur rare flowers ever bloom;
But fairer, dearer, Scotland's heath,
   An' bonny yellow broom :
The singing burn, the lowly cot
   Whaur first ye soucht my hand,
Than a' the flowers or gems that deck
   Bright India's fabled land.

I oft hae heard my father say,
   Langsyne, when by his hearth,
True love could bless the lowliest cot
   That ever rose on earth.
Now, here his honoured ashes lie,
   An' a' my pedigree;
Then dinna drag me frae the spot
   Sae hallow'd, love, tae me.

The Piedmont Glen—its flowery braes—
   The sacred trysting tree—
How can I leave those witching haunts,
   Sae dear to thee and me?
Whaur every bird, an' burn, an' bush,
   I ken by sicht an' name—
"Oh! say nae mair, my Mysie dear,
   I'll bide content at hame."

## LINES SUGGESTED BY THE CLOSING YEAR.

ADDRESSED TO W—— B——.

The dirge of Fifty-nine's been sung
By Time's truth-telling iron tongue,
Sae frae its frosty winds secure,
That rattle at my humble door,
A moment let me briefly scan
The moral, social state o' Man,
And see if Politics can cure
The many ills the poor endure,
Or if a name can change a man,
Or alter Nature's changeless plan,
Which maks some hearts be kind and leal,
And hardens ithers up like steel.

I have known men, Sir,—so have you—
Who off the poor the face did screw;
Who never did commiserate
The wandering beggar's wretched state;

Who never felt a pitying glow
Steal through their hearts for want or woe;
Who seized upon each trick or chance
Their sordid interests to advance;
Who did chicane and speculate
Until they earned each good man's hate;
And then before a gaping world
Their Liberal policy unfurled;
Men loud in their Reforming cry,
Whose whole life was a living lie,
As far as Liberty's defined
By heavenly or by human mind;'
Men who, if "Tories" call'd, would start,
Though not from principle or heart;
Yea, greedy as a rav'ning shark,
The "Liberal" Whigs—G–d save the mark!

And then there's men, you'll quite agree,
Who never prate o' liberty;
Aye ready wi' their purse or han'
To help their helpless brither man,
Or shed the sympathetic tear,
The drooping cheerless heart tae cheer;

In every man they see a friend
From tyranny they would defend;
Their liberty, like light from heaven,
Is meant for all—to all is given;
The man that's kind, good will remain,
Although a "Tory" be his name;
We canna change inherent nature
By ony clap-trap nomenclature.

As clouds and sunshine mix together
In April's variable weather,
So vice and virtue often meet
Upon the city's crowded street.
Some grub for siller through the gutters;
If heart they ha'e, its gold it mutters;
They ne'er tak up wi' ocht that's waff,
But say their prayers tae Aaron's calf.

Some spend their "summer while 'tis May,"
Unmindful of a winter day;
It comes at last with chilling air,
And leaves them standing leafless, bare;
Within the workhouse, sad, alone,

They find a house, but not a home;
Shed many a tear, heave many a sigh,
Till death appears, and then " good-bye"
To kind Inspector, sin, and folly,
Bad usage, hunger, melancholy.
Forbid it, every heavenly power,
That ever I should cross the door
Which separates the man and wife
When tottering on the verge o' life:
Expediency may say it's right,
But is it so in Heaven's sight?


Some marry young, syne propagation,
The pest o' folk in lowly station,
Soon swarms their hames wi' toddling bairns,
Could eat mair than the gudeman earns;
The wife turns heartless, thriftless, dirty,
The look o' her or house wad hurt ye;
The husband comes hame often tipsy,
Syne she fa's on him like a gipsy,
Heaps on his head fierce imprecations,
And he retorts wi' execrations,

Till Satan's black vocabulary
Is quite expended in their fury.

The children view, wi' streaming e'en,
The savage, fierce, unchristian scene,
Till repetition blunts their senses,
And then ye ken the consequences.
God help the children of such poor,
Let mercy open wide her door,
And underneath her sheltering wings
Protect the helpless wee bit things.

Some cry to lower the Franchise down
To every man o' judgment sound,
And then they can reduce taxation,
And that's the way tae help the nation;
Whilst Capital, wi' loud gaw-faw,
At this proposal wags its jaw,
It kens it has them in its claw,
And means, the fiend, tae swallow a'.

John Bright, thou Liberal rising star!
Oh, had ye power like Russia's Czar,

Ye ha'e the true Manchestrian heart
Would make the Landed Gentry start;
Would desecrate each bonny stream
Wi' motive-power, coal-reek, and steam;
Submerge the earth, and dwell in vapour,
To let the labouring poor live cheaper.
And pray, John Bright, your next move then?
"Why, work for less, my humble friend."
I know thee, John; thy noble race
Have gi'en me many a kind embrace;
Tae me and mine they kindly lent
Their cash at twenty-five per cent.;
For which I hope ye'll yet be knighted,
When Whiggery a' our wrangs has righted.

Tae mend these ills I speak anent,
Men cast their eyes tae Parliament;
A fool's eyes wander o'er the earth,
They never look around their hearth;
And there concealed the evils lie
Which legislative acts defy.
As well petition moon or sun
No more their radiant course to run,

As think our country's legislators
Can change our vices or our natures.
A moral law they canna pass,
And that is wanted maist, alas!
For ony party, state, or class.
Good laws may smooth the rugged road
Surrounding Labour's mean abode:
May give facilities to trade,
Protect what honesty has made,
But still our weal or woe depends
More on our conduct than our friends.

# GRANU TO HER SON.

### A FENIAN WELCOME.

RE-STRING me the ould harp ov Erin again,
An' play me, dear Paddy, some wild warlike strain;
Since the Fenians are coming, my darlint gossoon,
We must welcome the heroes wid some martial tune.

Ould "Lillybolero"—you mustn't try that,
It was played by the *Dutchman*—bad luck to him—Pat;
Since he trode on the shamrock, the black-hearted thief—
I'm sitting in sackcloth an' dying wid grief.

To uproot his offspring what schemes we have laid!
To shoot thim at midnight was part ov the trade—
The Whitefeet and Blackfeet tried that to get free,
But they caught thim an' hung thim like rogues on a tree

Dear, well I remimber the year ninety-eight—
Ohon! our afflictions were then very great;
But had we been thrue to each other thin, dear,
We would have been free from Fair Head to Cape Clear.

But the Saxons sent over big bagfuls ov gould,
An' for guineas, ma boughal, your counthry was sould;
Black Ballinahinch saw our standard laid low—
The Saxons rejoicing, your mother in woe.

When Daniel O'Connell arose in his might,
Och! hard did he labour to put things to right;
But he died broken-hearted, dear, list'ning our groans—
Leaving Rome his thrue heart, an' poor Ireland his bones.

Bould Meagher an' Mitchel they both sint away
To dhream of republics in Botany Bay;
At M'Cormick's back-door, where big cabbages grew,
They seized brave O'Brien, the treacherous crew!

Whin the Fenians come, Pat, across the salt say,
I hope they wont land, dear, at Bantry Bay;
Whin last our Frinch friends arrived at that spot,
They got a reciption uncommonly hot.

Strike up "Garryowen," thin, my darlint agra,
An' welcome the Fenians to Erin-go-bragh;
The Saxons may beat us, but still we can thry,
An' if we don't conquer, we know how to—fly.

## ARRAN.

The wildwood rose that blooms in June
    By wandering stream is fair to see;
And precious is the rich perfume
    The clover sheds upon the lea;
But Arran's heathy hills for me—
    The rifted rock, the roaring linn,
That make the mountains shout wi' glee,
    As o'er the rocks the waters spin.

Glen Cloy has countless charms untold,
    Unknown, unsung in lowland song;
Here Flora doth her charms unfold,
    And sunbeams love to linger long;
Here crystal waters ever sing
    Their joyous song of liberty—
Had I a choice, I would be king
    Of Arran's glens and mountains hie.

I seek not fame, but happiness;
    I sigh not for a lordly pile;
My prayer is—"Give me only this—
    A humble home in Arran's Isle."
There, blest with Jessie's sunny look,
    I'd sit beneath some ancient tree
That casts its shadow o'er the brook,
    And never prates of pedigree.

But night descends on Goatfell hoar;
    I hear "the Earl's" warning bell;
Again we seek Ardrossan's shore—
    To Arran's hills a sad farewell.
To-night my dreams go o'er the sea;
    For oh! to me the Isle is dear—
I tread its soil with ecstasy,
    And leave it often with a tear.

## LINES ON THE ERECTION OF GEN. NEILL'S MONUMENT AT AYR.

A tear for him who nobly fell,
    Far from a home and nation;
Alas! brave Neill, ye earned it well—
    This heartfelt, deep ovation.
When treason did the East enshroud
    With crimes dark and alarming,
Thy daring deeds dispelled the cloud
    At Lucknow's famous storming.

The British Lion flaunted high,
    Dark Bramah's sons defying;
While Azrael's wings obscured the sky,
    Above the dead and dying.
Amidst the deafening shout and cheer
    Of British heroes forming,
He fell, but not without a tear,
    At Lucknow's glorious storming.

No more by winding Ayr he'll stray,
   Amidst its beauties dreaming
Of battle-fields far, far away,
   With glory o'er them streaming.
His dreams are o'er, now cold in death
   He sleeps by Jumna's river,
But fame has bound a fadeless wreath
   Around his name for ever.

Though o'er his grave, in India's clime,
   May tread the savage stranger,
His country still will bear in mind
   Brave Neill, Cawnpore's avenger.
The whispering winds that kiss the wave
   Across the ocean flying,
Will softly murmur o'er his grave
   Our love unchanged, undying.

# SUMMER.

Welcome, Summer, with thy sunshine,
    Flowers and foliage, fruits and grain,
Blooming hedgerows crowned with woodbine,
    Breathing fragrance o'er the plain.

Now the humble star-like daisy
    Lifts its lowly dew-dimmed eye
To its wondrous brilliant likeness
    High above it in the sky.

Swallows swiftly skim the meadow,
    And the blackbird fills the glen
With the music of his woodnotes,
    Waking echo's voice again.

O'er his sleeping unfledged nestlings
    Nods the golden-tasselled broom,
While he serenades their slumbers
    With the melody of tune.

Theirs the truly regal palace,
    Grander than the monarch's home,
Lovely earth its flowery carpet,
    Starry heaven its glittering dome.

In the distant North horizon
    Slowly sinks the sun from view,
As a lover fondly lingers
    Ere he speaks the word, Adieu!

Now around the rural cottage
    Children meet to laugh and play;
Age looks on, amused, delighted,
    With the sports that close the day.

In the city's dingy alleys
    Pale-faced children raise their eyes
To the smoky-clouded curtain
    That obscures the Summer skies.

There the wretched mother wanders
    Through obscurity and din,
Seeking for her outcast offspring—
    Finds them in the haunts of sin.

Thou who saidst the little sparrow
    Did not fall unheeded down,
Look with Fatherly compassion
    On the children of the town.

Guard them from the foul contagion
    Of intemperance, vice, and crime;
Teach them that in truth and virtue
    Peace and happiness they'll find.

And when, forced by legislation,
    Capital must give a day,
Then away to stream and mountain,
    Where health-giving breezes play.

There the gems that deck creation,
    Teeming from the flowery sod,
Lifts the heart in adoration
    To the power that formed it—GOD!

## ADDRESS OF LORD G—'S TENANTRY.

My Lord,

 Tae us your honour is sae dear,
 We thought it proper tae appear
 In print, your character to clear
  Frae foul aspersion,
 And let folk ken, baith far and near,
  There's nae coercion.

 This curs'd Election is a bore,
 Our hearts are troubl'd unco sore,
 Tae think that we maun stan' before
  Baith frien' and fae,
 An' thole the taunts o' Jamie's core;
  It's hard we say.

 Forbye, Buchanan's prying crew,
 They're sure to sift the matter through,

An' haud it up to public view,
    And jeer an' lark it:
There's naething in his paper true,
    Except the Market.

An' then he sneers about our tacks,
An' criticises a' your acts,
An' says some wicked Landlord racks
    Puir farming bodies,
Unless they poll wi' them in packs,
    Like common cuddies.

The folk nae doubt will think it strange,
Tae see us vote against Sir James;
But, then, his conduct did estrange
    The love ye bore him;
An' when we saw your Lordship change,
    We did abhor him.

Now, here, we solemnly declare,
(Nay, if ye doubt, we're safe to swear,)
We're free as ony ane in Ayr
    Tae vote for Jamie;
But it wad be unkind, unfair,
    Tae gang again' ye.

Quite true, your Factor acted keen,
An' said the thing ye didna mean;
Ye ken Sir Charlie was your frien'
    Langsyne in Ayr;
For mony a day wi' tearfu' een
    Ye mourn'd him sair.

The folk o' Ayr may growl an' whine,
An' say ye're acting mean, unkind,
But we say ye dae richt tae mind
    The grave offence
O' gaun tae Derby's house tae dine,
    *It shews your sense.*

Now here wi' you we tak' our stan',
We'll clip the wings o' Jamie's clan;
Our services ye may comman'
    Against your foes;
But, hide the string within your han'
    That's through our nose.

    SIGNED ON BEHALF OF THE TWENTY-SIX,
        A NON-ELECTOR.

# JEANIE MOFFAT.

If Jeanie smiles, the warl may frown,
   I carena for its wayward thraws,
Nor how the slippery toy gaes round
   That fickle fortune queerly ca's.
Let ithers struggle in the cause
   That leads to worldly wealth and fame,
I'm careless quite whate'er befa's,
   Unless she cheers my cosie hame.

By Clutha's stream, in nichtly dreams,
   I wi' my winsome Jeanie stray;
But morning, wi' its rosy beams,
   Aye drives her bonny face away.
Then, oh, I canna speak by day
   The thochts, the words, I should impart;
Neist time we meet, I'll try to say
   How dear she's to my waiting heart.

The wild rose twines around the thorn;
 Beneath their shade the birdies pair;
The sportive hare that crops the corn
 Aye gets a mate his joys to share;
But I by Clutha roam forlorn,
 And breathe my vows to empty air;
Far better I had ne'er been born,
 Unless I win my Jeanie fair.

Oh, Jeanie Moffat, wad ye see
 Your lover leave his native hame,
In some strange land to pine and dee,
 Unkent to honour, love, and fame?
Ye'll sairly rue when I am gane
 For ever o'er the stormy sea;
Then say, oh say, ye'll be my ain,
 An' fill my heart wi' ecstacy.

## LORD EGLINTON'S BIRTH-DAY.

From Old Kilwinning's towers grey
Is many a banner streaming gay;
    Its merry bells do ring.
Long live the scion of a race
The County's ornament and grace,
    Amen doth Irvine sing.

Ardrossan sends across the bay
A greeting warm as this to-day
    To Eglinton's young chief:
May each returning birth-day bring
Peace, love, and joy upon its wing,
    Undimm'd by care and grief.

May ne'er misfortune's adverse gale
With sudden gust back-fill your sail,
 As o'er the waves ye glide
Of life's uncertain troubled sea;
With revelry upon your lee,
  Take prudence for your guide.

Avoid the swarm of Fashion's school
Who fish for joy in Folly's pool—
 Wise men have stumbled in;
When Pleasure's cover up ye beat,
Ye'll find her in some calm retreat,
 Afar from worldly din.

Long may you find in rural life
The peace that shuns the anxious strife
 Where competition reigns:
Still may the needy, helpless poor
Find succour at your Lordship's door,
 And bless your broad domains.

Still may the curling pond and green—
When curlers meet and bowlers keen—
 Be always graced by you;

The magic of Montgomery's name
Will give a zest to every game,
    Quite fascinating new.

Long may your huntsmen wake the morn
With baying hound and braying horn,
    By moorland, stream, and glen;
And children clap their hands and say—
" Lord Eglinton hunts here to-day
    With all his merry men."

## PADDY'S HALLUCINATIONS.

The cry of the *Nation* is always the same—
"Bad luck to the Saxons, confusion, and shame;"
It swears that ould Ireland like Eden would smile
If the heretic varmin were banished the Isle.
No longer would Pat have to wander abroad,
To work amongst mortar and carry the hod,
But sing in his hovel of mud, filth, and straw,
The beautiful ditties of Erin-go-bragh.

Whatever misfortunes to Paddy befal,
He dreams that the Saxons occasion them all;
His praties are blighted—in vain doth he toil—
While their shadow, like mildew, falls black on the soil.
"Och! would great Napoleon come over some day,
And sweep the invaders right into the say;
We would then get living like princes, agra,
In the beautiful Island of Erin-go-bragh."

The foes of the Saxons, Pat hails them as friends;
To Affghans or Caffres he sympathy sends;
"Success to the cousin of sun, moon, and stars—
Saint Patrick defend the brave Chinese Hussars!"
But, ochone! they're defeated, his heart sunk again,
Till he heard of the war on the Crimean plain;
Then up went his hat with a noisy whirrah—
*Repail now or nivir* for Erin-go-bragh.


"Och, woe to the Saxons!—salt tears may they weep!
On Inkerman's mountain they're dying like sheep;"
Mikey read in the *Nation*, he tould me last night,
They're stickin' in snow-wreaths an' haven't a bite.
We'll now purge the Island of heresy's sin—
Stop, Paddy, the massacre don't yet begin;
Nor throw up your brown, brimless hat, stuffed with straw,
There's luck, sure, in leisure, my darlint agra.


At last Nana Sahib arose in the East,
Producing a scene on which devils might feast;
Pat welcomed the tidings—they whispered relief—
But his joy, like the race of the hero, was brief.

Yet thousands in Ireland lament o'er the same,
Who would die to defend Britain's honour and fame;
"But, then, for Repail, sure they don't care a straw,
Or they'd welcome the devils to Erin-go-bragh."

Oh! Paddy cease dreaming, and turn up the sod;
The earth, sure, is faithful to Pagans abroad,
Who ne'er breathed a pater to Heaven, we're told,
Yet the tempting fruit hangs on the bushes like gold.
The Saxon and Celt are alike in God's sight;
To bless and to aid all is Heaven's delight—
Then let us be kind to each other, agra,
And imitate Heaven in Erin-go-bragh.

## THE SUN HAD PRESSED HIS OCEAN BED.

The sun had pressed his ocean bed
    Behind yon Arran hills,
And radiantly the moon had shed
    Her silver o'er the rills;
And far the Western waves did gleam
    Beneath her queenly eye;
While at my feet fair Girvan stream,
    Like music, glided by.

Its waters seemed to sing to me
    O' bygane happy days,
When, as the winds, I wandered free
    Upon its sunny braes;
Or wi' my Annie socht the shade
    Wi' woodbine overgrown,
Whaur many a flower its bloom displayed
    Around her wildwood throne.

But vanished are those joyous hours,
    For youth has passed away,
When fancy wove in fragrant bowers
    Its visions bright as day.
Gone is the loving heart sincere
    That blest my humble home;
Gone are the friends to memory dear—
    Earth gave them all a tomb.

The leafless tree upon the brae
    May brave bleak Winter's blasts,
Till Summer comes wi' sunshine gay,
    And verdure o'er it casts;
But joy to me will ne'er return,
    My lonely heart to cheer,
Until I meet the friends I mourn
    In some mair happy sphere.

## KILKERRAN'S BONNY BRAES.

By classic Doon the Minstrel sung
    O' winsome lasses braw;
But there is ane on Girvan's stream
    That's fairer than them a'.
There's no a flower by hill or glen
    That Simmer bright displays,
Can rival Edith Fergusson,
    On sweet Kilkerran's braes.

Young Jamie won her gentle hand,
    Syne brocht her to his ha',
To cast her shadow o'er our path,
    By mountain, stream, and shaw;
Whaur gracefu' as the sportive fawn
    That through the woodland strays,
She blesses wi' her joyous smiles
    Kilkerran's bonny braes.

The winning graces o' her mind—
    Love, innocence, and truth—
Will still our hearts towards her draw,
    When gone the charms o' youth.
And as the stars their radiance shed,
    To light earth's darksome ways,
Sae these will cheer the cheerless heart,
    Make bright Kilkerran's braes.

## LINES WRITTEN ON BURNS' ANNIVERSARY.

We meet in memory of the great
    Departed Bard of Scotia's land,
Whose noble strains yet sound as sweet
    As Ocean on Ardrossan's strand.
To hail the genius, rare and grand,
    That classic Coila well may boast,
Whose deathless notes in echoes sweet
    To-night are ringing round the coast.

We meet to drink the pathos deep,
    That from his peerless pen did flow;
To honour Ayrshire's princely son,
    That deeply felt another's woe.

And though the Minstrel lieth low,
    His spirit yet pervades this hall,
And comes, with memories of the past,
    To cheer the hearts of one and all.


Where is the man who never felt
    His heart respond to "Auld Langsyne,"
As up it conjured youthful days,
    When woman's face appeared divine?
And Scotland would disown the son
    Whose soul impassive could remain,
As Bruce harangues his mountaineers
    On Bannockburn's glorious plain.


Old azure Ocean may grow grey,
    The stars may lose their pristine light,
The Cannon Hill may pass away,
    That o'er us grandly looms to-night;
But Burns' poesy will live
    Through countless ages yet unborn—
Will laugh with those that merry are,
    And weep with those that weary mourn.

Long may Ardrossan's sons unite
    To hold the Bard's nativity,
And at the flame their tapers light
    Of soul-inspiring poesy.
In after ages may they beam,
    Like sunlight on the mountains grey,
Emitting rays of truth divine
    To cheer their children's weary way.

# SHAM FIGHT AT POLLOC.

Saint Mungo, what a glorious sight
Of waving plumes and armour bright,
   On Polloc field appears!
The smiling sun looks on the scene,
Enraptured with the martial mien
   Of Scotland's Volunteers.

Beyond the margin of the stream,
On Corker's Hill their bayonets gleam
   Like stars that gem the night;
But no life-stream will stain to-day
The Cart upon its peaceful way,
   For friendly is the fight.

Like rushing waters' distant hum,
From ancient Glasgow on they come,
   The thoughtless, sober, gay;

Some roll in silks and crinoline,
And others anything but fine,
   To view the grand display.

The bravery and the might are there
Of famed Dumbarton, bonny Ayr,
   Of Lanark and Renfrew;
All hail to Freedom's valiant band!
The guardians of our native land—
   The gallant and the true!

The peasant and the knight are there,
The winsome lass, the lady fair,
   To see the bloodless war;
To view, at least in mimic strife,
How Britons fought for home and life,
   On battle-fields afar.

To look upon the Greys again,
Who swept o'er Balaklava's plain
   Amidst a shower of death;
Who on the field of Waterloo
The chivalry of France o'erthrew,
   And won Fame's fadeless wreath.

Cold, base the heart must be indeed,
That would not wish the men God-speed
   Who fought in many a clime;
Who clipt the Gallic Eagle's wing,
And sent Napoleon, lone, to sing
   Ambition's parting hymn.

In columns vast, in proud array,
The gallant Volunteers display
   How glory may be won;
They fire, advance, retreat, re-form,
Amidst a lurid powdery storm,
   Obscuring earth and sun.

But hark! the trumpet's martial bray
Recalls the strugglers, from the fray,
   To pass in grand review;
The brave who fought on many a field,
The valiant Douglas, Grant, M'Neill,
   And others quite as true.

With men like these around our home,
Then let the foemen onward come
   In legions o'er the sea;

They'll guard the hallowed land of Bruce,
The land of liberty and truth,
   The haunts of chivalry.

At last, ascending to the skies,
We hear Victoria's anthem rise
   Amidst vociferous cheers;
And homeward as they wend their way,
They sing this patriotic lay—

"The British Volunteers."

   Should foreign foes menace us
      On Caledonia's strand,
   They never will disgrace us,
      The guardians of our land.
   But fight for home and beauty,
      For all that love endears,
   Like soldiers do their duty—
      The British Volunteers.

   Should Europe league together,
      And come across the waves,
   Our blood must dye the heather
      Before their power enslaves

The brave descendants of the Bruce,
  Whose spirit yet appears
To guard the land he trod in youth,
  Like Britain's Volunteers.

Unconquered Britons guard the Isle
  The world could ne'er subdue,
And glory ever loves to smile
  Upon the bonnets blue.
Then never shall a foeman tread
  The land that Fame reveres,
While Scotland's Thistle waves her head
  Above her Volunteers.

## LINES WRITTEN ON THE OPENING OF THE GIRVAN RAILWAY.

Time rolleth on, and changeth all
    That's mutable upon the earth;
Its onward silent footsteps fall
    Alike on poor and rich man's hearth.

Look at the past—for war array'd
    The Baron's bold retainers stand;
His lordly will must be obey'd,
    None dare dispute their chief's command.

Then Girvan's sweet secluded vale
    Was oft the scene of deadly feuds;
And many a crime we now bewail
    Awoke the Dryads of its woods.

The echoes which since then have slept
    In death-like silence by its stream,
Have woke to life with echoing beat,
    And hail their liberator—Steam.

Now Barons meet, but not in wrath,
   They differ still, but yet agree
Unitedly to smooth the path
   That leads to social harmony;

In aiding science to dispel
   The ignorance of ages past,
And o'er the land we love so well
   Its multifarious blessings cast.

Let pale-faced labour come and see
   The sun sink in his ocean bed,
And hear the wild waves' minstrelsy
   When clouds envelope Ailsa's head.

There see the sea-fowl go to rest
   Upon its cloud-lodged hoary peak;
While surging round their airy nests,
   The Western waves like thunder break.

The Northern coast of Erin's Isle
   Seen piled up to the Southern sky,
While gently, as a sleeping child,
   The azure Ocean now doth lie.

## LINES ON THE OPENING OF THE GIRVAN RAILWAY.

Fair Arran ! land of Highland hearts,
    Its verdant slopes, its Goatfell bare;
The great sun kisseth, and departs
    From view in golden glory there.

Then leave the city's smoky gloom,
    Its competition and its strife ;
Kilkerran's braes are now in bloom,
    Bargany's wild woods teem with life.

Around Killochan's ancient hall
    The wild flowers sweetly scent the air,
The rook's hoarse notes at evening fall
    Are heard amongst the old trees there.

The land of Carrick—home of Bruce,
    Who fought, and won our liberty ;
The land of song, of love, and truth :
    Come down by rail this land and see.

## LINES ON THE DEATH OF CAPTAIN WILSON.

Sit here, beside the Castle wall
    That's mouldering fast away,
Where ivy loves to darkly crawl
    O'er ruin and decay:
Here oft he gazed at evening tide,
Enraptured on the swelling Clyde.

He loved the waves; they were his home
    In manhood's morning day;
He gloried still to see their foam
    Break o'er the Horse Isle, grey,
Or chase each other o'er the sand
Along Ardrossan's shelly strand.

But yesterday his accents sweet
    Did gladden street and home;
To-day the earth's his winding sheet,
    Within the silent tomb;
But still affection seeks his grave,
Its agonizing griefs to rave.

The trembling dew-drops on the grass,
    That glisten o'er his bed,
But symbolize the tears, alas!
    By many for him shed.
The generous friend, forgiving foe—
Oh death, why didst thou lay him low?

Eternity's dark waters lave
    The land where all are free,
When safe across its noiseless wave
    We'll hold a jubilee—
An intellectual feast of love
With Wilson in the realms above.

## THE COTTON FAMINE.

Dark dreary December has spread o'er the earth
    Its mantle of mistyness, woven by gloom,
And Want has sat down on the working-man's hearth,
    As pale as the spectres that tenant the tomb.

The factories are silent, their shuttles are still,
    Their life has departed, their cotton is gone;
And swift as a torrent descends from a hill,
    Fierce famine has fastened on many a one.

Mementoes of friendship, heirlooms of the past,
    The ring of betrothal,—all's gone to the pawn;
Yet bravely they battle adversity's blast—
    God hasten prosperity's bread-giving dawn!

Let peace spread her wings o'er Columbia's shore,
    The world is weary of madness and strife;
The North bent on conquest—they fight for no more—
    The South for their homesteads, their honour, and life.

Democracy stalketh in blood o'er the land,
   Misrule and oppression roll on as a wave,
Submerging whatever is noble in man,
   Invoking the hatred of master and slave.

The star-spangled banner is now rent in twain,
   In tatters it droops over Liberty's grave;
There's few but John Bright would unite it again,
   Or Leatham—he's silly—the other's a knave.

They'd have us succumb to the men we despise;
   Ask pardon of those who but merit disdain;
" No, rather starvation," brave Lancashire cries,
   " Our banner's unsullied, so let it remain."

God strengthen those heroes, and God bless the men
   Who rushed to the rescue of Lancashire's sons;
" A Derby for ever," shouts Britain again,
   More loud than the roll of Republican guns.

With such men to aid us, we may rest secure,
   Tho' Famine's pale foot-prints are seen on the strand;
Their thousands will frighten the wolf from the door,
   Till cotton is gathered in some other land.

## LINES ON A TOMBSTONE IN ARDROSSAN CEMETERY.

How peacefully they slumber here,
Removed from sorrow, sin and fear,—
Till Christ shall in his glory come
And take them to his blissful home—
A land more lovely far than this,
Of seraph song and endless bliss.

www.ingramcontent.com/pod-product-compliance
Lightning Source LLC
Chambersburg PA
CBHW020816230426
43666CB00007B/1036